Welcome to a...
Country Woman Christmas

I t's a time to cherish merry memories—and create exciting new ones you'll hold dear for years.

There's no other season like Christmas. And there's no other book like the one you're holding right now.

You see, *Country Woman Christmas* is truly a celebration of Christmas from the heart of the country. Almost all the recipes, photos, stories and craft ideas you'll find here have come to us directly from the readers of *Country Woman* magazine.

This book includes everything you need to make your family's upcoming holiday celebration your happiest—and least hurried—ever.

Festive *Family* Food. From appetizers to desserts, this keepsake book brings you *90* never-before-published hearty recipes to add to your festive file. But these aren't just any recipes. Each had to pass a rigorous taste test in the *Country Woman* kitchen—and an equally important *time* test.

Country women are busy people at Christmastime, with no time to spare for extra trips to town. So—like those in *Country Woman* itself—*every* recipe in this book can be made with ingredients most cooks keep right on hand.

Quick Crafts, Too. Similarly, *Country Woman Christmas* contains dozens of original holiday craft projects—with complete instructions, patterns and charts—that take no more than a few hours to finish...yet will brighten your home and gift-giving long after this season ends!

You'll also enjoy cheerfully informative profiles of country women who find special ways to bring the holidays home, true stories of the beauty of Christmas, touching seasonal poems from country-loving and Christmas-loving folks just like you—and many other delightful features and photos.

Like What You See? Keep in mind that this is just the first in a series of annual *Country Woman Christmas* books. So there's *lots* more to look forward to in the years ahead.

For now, though, settle in and discover the unique joys of this *Country Woman Christmas*! ▲

Senior Editor
Kathy Pohl

Editor
Karen Thibodeau

Food Editor
Mary Beth Jung

Assistant Food Editor
Coleen Martin

Test Kitchen Home Economists
Rochelle Schmidt
Karla Spies

Test Kitchen Assistants
Judith Scholovich
Sherry Smalley

Craft Editor
Kathy Rankin

Associate Editors
Sharon Selz
Kristine Krueger
Kathy Mangold

Editorial Assistant
Ann Follansbee

Art Director
Linda Dzik

Assistant Art Director
Vicky Wilimitis

Art Associate
Nancy Krueger

Food Photography Artist
Stephanie Marchese

Photo Studio Coordinator
Anne Schimmel

Production Assistant
Judy Pope

© 1996 Reiman Publications, L.P.
5400 S. 60th Street
Greendale WI 53129

International Standard Book Number:
0-89821-171-9
Library of Congress Catalog Card Number:
96-67482

INSIDE...

AND MUCH MORE!

PICTURED ON OUR COVER. Clockwise from top center: Macaroon Kisses (p. 26) in Paper Twist Berry Basket (p. 68), Minty Hot Chocolate (p. 41), Knit Christmas Stocking (p. 100), Pulled Taffy Candy Canes (p. 33), Reindeer Cookies (p. 27), Fern-Stenciled Gift Wrap (p. 102), Poinsettia Cake, center (p. 42). Back cover: Edible Gingerbread House (p. 44).

Cover, Craft and Food Photography: Scott Anderson; **Other Photo Contributors:** p. 3—Martha McBride/Unicorn Stock Photos, p. 4—Fred Preisler/Unicorn Stock Photos, p. 6—Dick Dietrich, p. 7—Woody Metzger/Rich Frutchey Associates, p. 49—Bruce Blank, p. 69—David Wilson, p. 70—H. Schmeiser/Unicorn Stock Photos, p. 71—Robin Adams, p. 74—John McKeith, p. 75—Dede Hatch, p. 89—Fred D. Jordan/Unicorn Stock Photos, p. 90—Gerry Haynie, p. 92—Anthony Shaw, p. 110—Mary Markley, Clark Gilbert, Lynne Gilbert, p. 113—Terry Barner/Unicorn Stock Photos.

Readers' Poetry Corner

Christmas Memories

Christmas memories through the years
That bring the greatest pleasure
Are not of costly gifts received
But simple things we treasure:

The warmth from a crackling fireplace,
A sleigh ride through pristine snow,
The sound of church bells echoing
Through hills and valleys below.

The fragrant scent of fresh pine boughs,
Colorful lights on the tree,
Lovers kissing 'neath mistletoe,
Voices joined in harmony.

It's sharing with those around us
A magical time of year
When we greet both friends and strangers
With wishes of Yuletide cheer.

May the blessings of the season
And the joys that they impart
Touch your life with countless wonders
That remain within your heart.
—**Ruth Fiori Poynor**
Boise, Idaho

Christmas Cookie Magic

There is in childhood's treasure chest
A custom I remember best—
The special yearly family treat
When we baked Christmas cookies sweet.

An expert cook, Mom cast her spell,
Her students creamed and sifted well.
The room became a magic place,
We watched Mom mix and knead with grace.

Then every child, bright eyes aglow,
Rolled flat a precious bit of dough,
Cut out well-chosen shapes with care
In spicy fragrant Christmas air.

As cookies into oven went,
Our mouths all watered at the scent…
Till out they came a welcome sight,
Quite golden brown and baked just right.

Then each of us would sample one
The very minute they were done,
And frost the Santa, Christmas tree,
Bell, star and reindeer shapes with glee.

In modern kitchen I recall
Our cookie fun when I was small,
Get out Mom's favorite recipes
And plan to make some memories.
—**Louise Pugh Corder**
Franklinville, North Carolina

Fruits of Baker's Christmas Labors Are Naturally Good

HOW GOOD is the locally flavored fruitcake Mary Ormrod cooks up for the holidays around Cavendish, Vermont? Well, after just one taste, her boss offered to hand his business over to her—and he's a baker!

"Lots of people say, 'I *hate* fruitcake!'" Mary explains. "But they find themselves coming back to this one."

Mary was working at a bakery in Cavendish a decade ago when she presented her boss with a homemade fruitcake as a Christmas gift. He quickly suggested she take over the bakery—during its scheduled twice-a-year closings, that is—and turn out her from-scratch specialty in large quantity.

Now, with husband Andrew as her partner, Mary begins the painstaking baking process by chopping buckets of unsulfured dried apricots and prunes.

"Next, we weigh out raw cashews, raisins and walnuts...mix up quarts of pure Vermont honey, cream and eggs ...and add only enough flour to hold the cake together," she advises.

"After a long slow bake at 250°, we age the cakes for months at 40° in a home-built cooler in the basement of our log home."

Mary and Andrew do all of the work the old-fashioned way...by hand. Plus,

fresh ingredients—the eggs come from a local farmer and the honey from a nearby beekeeper, for instance—add a quality mass-produced cakes can't duplicate.

The Christmas spirit is what first focused the couple on fruitcake. "With family and friends in both the U.S. and Canada," Mary remembers, "we wanted to send holiday gifts that would survive the postal rush and still satisfy everyone. Fruitcake was the answer!"

Fittingly, given that close-knit start, Mary and Andrew's newest "employee" is their daughter Jade Lily. "She helps out mostly by 'supervising'," Mary merrily reports.

Lately, her 4-year-old eyes have been settling on more than fruitcake. With that seasonal success, Mary and Andrew have branched out to other products—including one called Vermont Volcano Mustard. Sounds like powerful stuff!

Editor's Note: *For information on ordering Mary's fruitcakes or other products, send a self-addressed stamped business-size envelope to Old Cavendish Products, Box 631, Cavendish VT 05142 or phone 1-800/536-7899.* ▲

SECRET INGREDIENT in Mary Ormrod's fruitcakes is old-fashioned, by-hand method. Booming business is family affair with husband Andrew (above) and their daughter, Jade Lily (top left).

WELCOME TO MY COUNTRY KITCHEN

By Sharman Neitzert of Huron, South Dakota

IT'S LONG been said that the heart of a country home is the kitchen. Well, here at *our* Christmas-loving place, my kitchen's also at the heart of holiday festivities!

My family—husband Jack and children Brandon, 15, and Corey, 10—likes to celebrate Christmas with heaps of homemade touches. So, as the season approaches, I spend lots of time whipping up Yule treats. Generally, I can count on Jack and the boys to assume prime goody-snitching positions at the breakfast counter! That spacious surface is also handy for crafting homemade gifts for family and friends.

Actually, with its year-round theme built around my favorite color of red, my kitchen has a head start on Christmas spirit. The warm hue—with country blue countertops and accents—stands out in my printed heart wallpaper and border. Red-and-white curtains, chair cushions, place mats, rugs and more carry that theme through to the adjacent dining area.

To ring the entire room with a jolly naturalness, I drape an evergreen swag over the kitchen doorway. Around the corner, Santa perches on top of an overflowing red wooden sleigh Jack cut out for me (leading the way, needless to say, is Rudolph the Red-Nosed Reindeer!). Meanwhile, from a mirrored oak shelf above, a collection of Santas, snowmen and reindeer peers down.

Spreading the season's sunny spirit even farther, I spruce up my honey oak cabinets with more greenery garlands and mini poinsettias. That Christmasy combination is a happy complement to my teapot collection, housed on top of the cabinets. (It includes some family heirlooms as well as souvenirs from fondly remembered vacations.)

Of course—along with baskets of poinsettias, wicker sleighs, angels and other craft-show treasures—there's a spot reserved for Mr. and Mrs. Claus…a snowy site on the kitchen bookshelf.

Other lively and lighthearted visitors gather in the nearby dining area when we entertain. For those neighborly occasions, the table's topped off with an evergreen centerpiece I crafted and plenty of Christmas-colored candles. I also season the setting with a festive red tablecloth and felt poinsettia napkin rings—a *Country Woman* craft project from a few years ago.

This year, it's been a pleasure sharing my holiday kitchen with you. I hope having a look at its cheerful touches made this sparkling season brighter yet for you…and maybe even gave you a few ideas for your own kitchen. Merry Christmas! ▲

IN THE CHRISTMAS SPIRIT! Country kitchen of Sharman Neitzert (shown at left with husband Jack, sons Brandon and Corey) is decked in festive finery in every corner. Above, Yule dining's in good taste, too!

BEAUTIFUL BRUNCH! Starting clockwise from top right: Glazed Doughnuts (p. 11), Breakfast in Bread (p. 12), Mix 'n' Match Quiche (p. 11), Winter Fruit Bowl (p. 11) and Citrus Punch (p. 12).

Holiday Brunch

*Make your holiday gathering extra special
with these festive crowd-pleasers.*

WINTER FRUIT BOWL
Margaret Schaeffer, Orlando, Florida
(Pictured on page 10)

This fruit salad goes well with any meat dish. The blend of grapefruit and cranberries gives it a tangy flavor—and a pretty holiday look.

    4 medium grapefruit
1/4 cup water
    1 cup sugar
1/2 cup orange marmalade
    2 cups fresh *or* frozen cranberries
    3 medium firm bananas, sliced

Peel and section grapefruit, removing membrane and reserving 1/4 cup juice. In a saucepan, combine water, sugar, marmalade and reserved grapefruit juice; bring to a boil over medium heat. Cook and stir until sugar dissolves. Add cranberries. Reduce heat to medium; simmer 8-10 minutes or until cranberries pop. Remove from the heat. Gently stir in grapefruit. Chill for at least 1 hour. Stir in bananas just before serving. **Yield: 8-10 servings.**

MIX 'N' MATCH QUICHE
From the *Country Woman* Test Kitchen
(Pictured on page 10)

Combine colorful crabmeat and asparagus to bake this hearty main dish that's both festive and flavorful—or choose your family's favorite ingredients…and create your own one-of-a-kind specialty! You'll be surprised at the compliments you'll receive.

    1 unbaked pastry shell (9 inches)
    1 can (6 ounces) crabmeat*, flaked and drained
    1 cup frozen asparagus cuts*, thawed
    2 tablespoons chopped onion
    2 tablespoons chopped sweet red pepper
    1 cup (4 ounces) shredded Swiss *or* cheddar
       cheese
    3 eggs
1-1/2 cups half-and-half cream
1/2 teaspoon salt
1/8 teaspoon pepper
1/8 teaspoon ground nutmeg

Do not prick pastry shell; line with a double thickness of heavy-duty foil. Bake at 450° for 5 minutes. Remove foil; bake 5 minutes more. Reduce heat to 325°. Layer crab, asparagus, onion, red pepper and cheese in crust. In a small bowl, beat eggs, cream, salt, pepper and nutmeg; pour over cheese. Bake for 35-45 minutes or until a knife inserted near the center comes out clean. Let stand 10 minutes before cutting. **Yield: 6-8 servings. *Editor's Note:*** You can mix and match ingredients to come up with your own personal quiche. For the crab, substitute 8 ounces of browned pork sausage or 1 cup of diced cooked chicken or ham. For the asparagus, substitute 1 cup of frozen broccoli or a broccoli-cauliflower-carrot blend.

GLAZED DOUGHNUTS
Pat Siebenaler, Westminster, Colorado
(Pictured on page 10)

The coffee-flavored glaze on these moist and tasty doughnuts makes them a perfect way to start off the morning…on Christmas Day or any day. You'll find this recipe is a great way to use up leftover potatoes.

    2 packages (1/4 ounce *each*) active dry yeast
1/4 cup warm water (110° to 115°)
    2 cups warm milk (110° to 115°)
1/2 cup butter *or* margarine
    1 cup hot mashed *or* riced potatoes
       (without added butter or seasoning)
    3 eggs
1/2 teaspoon lemon extract, optional
    1 cup sugar
1-1/2 teaspoons salt
1/2 teaspoon ground cinnamon
9-1/4 to 9-3/4 cups all-purpose flour
COFFEE GLAZE:
    6 to 8 tablespoons cold milk
    1 tablespoon instant coffee granules
    2 teaspoons vanilla extract
3/4 cup butter *or* margarine, softened
    6 cups confectioners' sugar
1/2 teaspoon ground cinnamon
Pinch salt
Cooking oil for deep-fat frying

In a large mixing bowl, dissolve yeast in water. Add milk, butter, potatoes, eggs and extract if desired. Add sugar, salt, cinnamon and 3 cups flour; mix well. Add enough remaining flour to form a soft dough. Cover and let rise in a warm place until doubled, about 1 hour. Stir down; roll out on a well-floured board to 1/2-in. thickness. Cut with a 2-1/2-in. doughnut cutter. Place on greased baking sheets; cover and let rise for 45 minutes. Meanwhile, for glaze, combine 6 tablespoons milk, coffee and vanilla; stir to dissolve coffee. In a bowl, combine butter, sugar, cinnamon and salt; mix well. Gradually add milk mixture; beat until smooth, adding additional milk to make a dipping consistency. In an electric skillet or deep-fat fryer, heat oil to 350°. Fry doughnuts, a few at a time, about 1-1/2 minutes per side or until golden. Drain on paper towels. Dip tops in glaze while warm. **Yield:** about 4 dozen.

• Keep holiday fruit punches chilled with a floating ice ring. Simply freeze water or fruit juice in a ring mold. For added color, arrange fruit in the liquid before freezing.

CITRUS PUNCH
Dianne Conway, London, Ontario
(Pictured on page 10)

This zesty punch is a refreshing addition to my holiday table. I love its fruity flavor and the bright sunshiny color. You can easily double the recipe if you're expecting a larger group.

    2 cups orange juice
    1 cup grapefruit juice
    2 cups pineapple juice
    1 cup lemonade
    2 cups ginger ale

Chill all ingredients; mix gently in a pitcher or punch bowl. **Yield:** 12-16 servings (2 quarts).

BREAKFAST IN BREAD
Joyce Brown, Warner Robins, Georgia
(Pictured on page 10)

I enjoy making this delicious bread since it's very easy and a nice change of pace from sweeter breads. It's a "never-fail" treat, and friends always ask for the recipe. The hearty ingredients make it a complete meal in one pan.

    6 eggs
1-1/2 cups all-purpose flour
2-1/2 teaspoons baking powder
    1/2 teaspoon salt
    3/4 cup milk
    6 bacon strips, cooked and crumbled
    1 cup diced fully cooked ham
    1 cup *each* shredded Monterey Jack, Swiss and
        sharp cheddar cheese

In a large bowl, beat eggs until foamy. Combine flour, baking powder and salt. Gradually add to eggs with milk; mix well. Stir in bacon, ham and cheeses. Pour into a greased 9-in. x 5-in. x 3-in. loaf pan. Bake at 350° for 50-60 minutes or until a wooden pick inserted near the center comes out clean and top is golden brown. Serve warm. **Yield:** 1 loaf. **Editor's Note:** Baked loaf may be frozen and reheated.

BRUNCH PIZZA
Janelle Lee, Sulphur, Louisiana

Whenever I entertain guests, this zippy pizza is a definite crowd-pleaser. (It also makes a great late-night snack for any time of the year!)

    1 pound bulk pork sausage
    1 tube (8 ounces) refrigerated crescent rolls
    1 cup frozen shredded hash browns
    1 cup (4 ounces) shredded cheddar cheese
    5 eggs
    1/4 cup milk
    1/2 teaspoon salt
    1/4 teaspoon pepper
    2 tablespoons grated Parmesan cheese

Cook and crumble sausage; drain and set aside. Separate crescent roll dough into eight triangles and place on an ungreased 12-in. round pizza pan with points toward center. Press over the bottom and up the sides to form a crust; seal perforations. Spoon sausage over crust; sprinkle with hash browns and cheddar cheese. In a bowl, beat eggs, milk, salt and pepper; pour over cheese. Sprinkle with Parmesan. Bake at 375° for 25-30 minutes or until crust is golden. **Yield:** 6-8 servings.

CHEERY CHERRY COMPOTE
Jeanee Volkmann, Waukesha, Wisconsin

I always get loads of compliments on this sweet, colorful compote with its variety of fruits when I serve it for holiday brunch. It's a quick and easy recipe that only looks like it requires hours to prepare in the kitchen.

2-1/2 cups water
    2 cups pitted prunes
1-1/2 cups dried apricots
    1 can (21 ounces) cherry pie filling
    1 can (20 ounces) pineapple chunks, undrained
    1/4 cup white grape juice
Lemon slices

In a large saucepan, bring water, prunes and apricots to a boil; reduce heat. Simmer, uncovered, for 10 minutes. Remove from the heat and let stand for 5 minutes; drain. Add pie filling, pineapple and grape juice; bring to a boil. Reduce heat; cover and simmer for 10 minutes or until fruit is tender. Let stand for 5 minutes. Serve warm; garnish with lemon slices. **Yield:** 10-12 servings.

HEARTY HAM CASSEROLE
Sharon Cobb, Fairfax, Vermont

I first made this filling casserole for a camping trip with friends, adding potatoes and soup to stretch the recipe. It was a big hit. It's a great all-in-one meal that's sure to please your hungry eaters all year-round.

    4 medium potatoes
    1 package (10 ounces) frozen chopped broccoli
    1/4 cup finely chopped onion
    3 tablespoons butter *or* margarine, *divided*
    1 tablespoon all-purpose flour
    1/8 teaspoon pepper
    1 cup milk
    1/2 cup shredded cheddar cheese
    2 cups cubed fully cooked ham
    1 can (10-3/4 ounces) condensed cream of
        mushroom soup, undiluted
    1/4 cup dry bread crumbs

Cook potatoes in boiling salted water until tender; drain. Peel and cube; set aside. Cook the broccoli according to package directions, omitting salt; drain and set aside. In a large skillet, saute onion in 2 tablespoons butter until tender. Add flour and pepper; stir until smooth. Gradually add milk; cook and stir until mixture boils and thickens. Remove from the heat; stir in cheese until melted. Stir in ham, soup, potatoes and broccoli. Transfer to a greased 2-1/2-qt. baking dish. Melt remaining butter; toss with the bread crumbs. Sprinkle over top of casserole. Bake, uncovered, at 350° for 20-30 minutes or until heated through. **Yield:** 6-8 servings.

Christmas Breads

*Served warm from the oven or given as tasty gifts,
these breads lend the holidays an old-fashioned feel.*

MAPLE NUT COFFEE CAKE
Rosadene Herold, Lakeville, Indiana
(Pictured on page 15)

Every time I make this coffee cake for the holidays or church functions, the pan is emptied in a hurry. People rave about it.

    1 package (16 ounces) hot roll mix
    3 tablespoons sugar
    3/4 cup warm water (120° to 130°)
    1 egg
    1 teaspoon maple flavoring
    1/2 cup butter *or* margarine, melted, *divided*
FILLING:
    1/2 cup sugar
    1 teaspoon ground cinnamon
    1/2 teaspoon maple flavoring
    1/3 cup chopped walnuts
GLAZE:
1-1/2 cups confectioners' sugar
    1/4 teaspoon maple flavoring
    1 to 2 tablespoons milk

In a large bowl, combine flour packet and yeast from hot roll mix. Add sugar. Stir in water, egg, flavoring and 6 tablespoons butter; mix well. Turn onto a floured board; knead until smooth and elastic, 2-3 minutes. Place in a greased bowl; turn once to grease top. Cover and let rise in a warm place until doubled, 45-60 minutes. For filling, combine sugar, cinnamon and flavoring. Add nuts; set aside. Divide dough into thirds. On a lightly floured surface, roll out one portion to a 12-in. circle; place on a greased 12-in. pizza pan. Brush with some of the remaining butter. Sprinkle with a third of the filling. Repeat, forming two more layers, ending with filling. Pinch dough around outer edge to seal. Mark a 2-in. circle in center of dough (do not cut through). Cut from outside edge just to the 2-in. circle, forming 16 wedges. Twist each wedge five to six times. Cover and let rise until doubled, 30-45 minutes. Bake at 375° for 20-25 minutes or until golden brown. Cool on a wire rack. Combine glaze ingredients; drizzle over warm coffee cake. **Yield:** 16 servings.

ST. NICHOLAS BREAD
Mabel Oen, De Forest, Wisconsin
(Pictured on pages 14 and 15)

I've been making this bread baked in a can for Christmas gifts for many years. Everyone loves its unique shape.

    1 cup coarsely chopped pecans
    1 cup raisins
    1 cup dried currants
    1 cup finely chopped dried apricots
    1 cup finely chopped mixed candied fruit
   10 to 11 cups all-purpose flour, *divided*
    2 packages (1/4 ounce *each*) active dry yeast
    1/2 cup warm water (110° to 115°)
    2 cups warm milk (110° to 115°)
    1 cup sugar
    1/2 cup plus 2 tablespoons butter *or* margarine, softened, *divided*
    2 eggs, lightly beaten
    1 tablespoon salt
    1 teaspoon ground cardamom
GLAZE:
1-1/2 cups confectioners' sugar
    1/2 teaspoon vanilla extract
    2 to 3 tablespoons milk
Candy sprinkles

Place the first five ingredients in a large bowl. Sprinkle with 1 cup of flour; toss and set aside. In a large mixing bowl, dissolve yeast in water. Add milk, sugar, 1/2 cup butter, eggs, salt, cardamom and 3 cups flour; beat until smooth. Add enough of the remaining flour to make a soft, slightly sticky dough. Blend in fruit mixture. Turn onto a floured board; cover and let rest 10 minutes. Knead until smooth and elastic, 6-8 minutes. Place in a greased bowl, turning once to grease top. Cover and let rise in a warm place until doubled, about 1-1/2 hours. Punch dough down. Divide into six pieces and shape into small round loaves; place in well-greased 13-oz. coffee cans. Brush tops with remaining butter. Cover and let rise in a warm place until doubled, about 1-1/2 hours. Bake at 350° for 45-55 minutes or until golden brown. Cool in cans 5 minutes before removing to wire racks; cool completely. For glaze, combine confectioners' sugar, vanilla and milk; drizzle over loaves. Decorate with candy sprinkles. **Yield:** 6 loaves.

PINEAPPLE BANANA BREAD
Stephanie Bates, Aiea, Hawaii
(Pictured on page 14)

This pretty loaf adds a tropical feel to any festive occasion. It's also a great way to use up your extra bananas.

    1/2 cup butter *or* margarine, softened
    1 cup sugar
    2 eggs
    1/2 cup mashed ripe banana
    1/3 cup drained crushed pineapple
    1/2 cup flaked coconut
    2 cups all-purpose flour
    1 teaspoon baking powder
    1/2 teaspoon baking soda
    1/2 teaspoon salt

In a mixing bowl, cream butter and sugar. Beat in eggs. Stir in banana, pineapple and coconut. Combine dry ingredients; stir into creamed mixture just until combined. Spoon into a greased 8-in. x 4-in. x 2-in. loaf pan. Bake at 350° for 65-70 minutes or until bread tests done. Cool in pan 10 minutes; remove to a wire rack. **Yield:** 1 loaf.

FESTIVE BREADS. Clockwise from top right: Cranberry Nut Muffins (p. 16), Maple Nut Coffee Cake (p. 13), Pineapple Banana Bread (p. 13), Candy Cane Bread (p. 16), St. Nicholas Bread (p. 13).

CRANBERRY NUT MUFFINS

Marianne Clarke, Crystal Lake, Illinois
(Pictured on page 15)

This special holiday bread recipe combines two of my favorites—tangy dried cranberries and spicy cardamom.

>   2 cups all-purpose flour
>   1 cup sugar
>   1 teaspoon baking soda
>   1 teaspoon ground cardamom
>   1 teaspoon ground cloves
>   1 cup buttermilk
>   1 egg
>   1/2 cup butter *or* margarine, melted
>   1/2 cup dried cranberries
>   1/2 cup chopped walnuts
> CARDAMOM BUTTER:
>   1/2 cup butter *or* margarine, softened
>   1/4 cup confectioners' sugar
>   1 teaspoon ground cardamom

In a bowl, combine the dry ingredients. Stir in buttermilk, egg, butter, cranberries and nuts just until moistened. Fill greased or paper-lined muffin cups three-fourths full. Bake at 400° for 20-25 minutes or until muffins test done. Cool in pans 10 minutes before removing to a wire rack. Beat cardamom butter ingredients until smooth; serve with muffins. **Yield:** 14 muffins and about 3/4 cup butter.

CANDY CANE BREAD

Marie Basinger, Connellsville, Pennsylvania
(Pictured on page 14)

A festive shape and Christmasy colors make this bread a hit at holiday time. Use cranberries for a zesty flavor, or substitute raisins or currants if you prefer.

> 5-1/2 to 6 cups all-purpose flour, *divided*
>   2 packages (1/4 ounce *each*) active dry yeast
>   1 teaspoon salt
>   1 cup milk
>   1/2 cup sugar
>   1/2 cup water
>   1/4 cup butter *or* margarine
>   2 eggs
>   2 tablespoons grated orange peel
> 1-1/2 cups dried cranberries, currants *or* raisins
> FILLING:
>   6 tablespoons butter *or* margarine, softened,
>   *divided*
>   3/4 cup packed brown sugar
> 1-1/2 teaspoons ground cinnamon
> GLAZE:
> 1-1/2 cups confectioners' sugar
>   1 teaspoon vanilla extract
>   1 to 2 tablespoons milk

In a large mixing bowl, combine 2-1/2 cups flour, yeast and salt; mix well. In a small saucepan, heat milk, sugar, water and butter until a thermometer reads 120°-130° (butter does not need to be melted). Pour into yeast mixture; add eggs and orange peel. Beat for 30 seconds, scraping bowl often. Beat on high for 3 minutes. Stir in cranberries and enough remaining flour to form a firm dough. Turn onto a floured board; knead until smooth and elastic, 6-8 minutes. Place in a greased bowl, turning once to grease top. Cover and let rise in a warm place until doubled, about 1 hour. Punch dough down. Divide into thirds. Roll one portion into a 12-in. x 9-in. rectangle. Spread with 2 tablespoons butter. Combine brown sugar and cinnamon; sprinkle a third over the butter. Roll up from a long end. Cut into 11 rolls; arrange in a candy cane shape on a large greased baking sheet. Repeat with remaining dough and filling. Cover and let rise until nearly doubled, about 30 minutes. Bake at 350° for 18-23 minutes or until lightly browned. Cool on a wire rack. Combine glaze ingredients; drizzle over canes. **Yield:** 3 breads.

MINI POPPY SEED LOAVES

Mrs. Richard Bridges, Absarokee, Montana

Each Christmas, I make plates of goodies for the neighbors. I try to include a few items that aren't as sweet as traditional cookies and candies—these mini loaves really fit the bill!

>   2 cups all-purpose flour
>   1 cup sugar
>   1 tablespoon poppy seeds
>   1 teaspoon grated lemon peel
>   1/2 teaspoon baking soda
>   1 cup (8 ounces) plain yogurt
>   1/2 cup butter *or* margarine, melted
>   2 eggs, beaten
>   1 teaspoon vanilla extract
>   1/2 teaspoon almond extract

In a bowl, combine flour, sugar, poppy seeds, lemon peel and baking soda. Combine remaining ingredients; stir into flour mixture just until moistened. Spoon into three greased 5-in. x 2-1/2-in. mini loaf pans. Bake at 350° for 25-30 minutes or until a wooden pick inserted near the center comes out clean. Cool on a wire rack. **Yield:** 3 loaves.

LEMON-DROP DINNER ROLLS

Jackie Johnson, Merrill, Wisconsin

My family loves these rolls with Christmas dinner. Their lemony flavor is a nice accompaniment to turkey and all the trimmings—or to my husband's favorite main course, beef roast. Using frozen bread dough helps save time during the holiday rush!

>   1 loaf (1 pound) frozen white *or* sweet bread
>   dough, thawed
>   1/4 cup sugar
> 4-1/2 teaspoons grated lemon peel
>   1/8 teaspoon ground nutmeg
>   2 tablespoons butter *or* margarine, melted

Divide dough into 12-18 pieces; shape into balls. In a small bowl, combine sugar, lemon peel and nutmeg. Dip tops of rolls into butter, then into sugar mixture. Place in greased muffin cups, sugar side up. Cut a 1/2-in.-deep cross on tops of rolls. Cover and let rise in a warm place until doubled, about 1-1/2 hours. Bake at 375° for 14-16 minutes or until golden brown. Immediately remove from pan; cool on wire racks. **Yield:** 1 to 1-1/2 dozen.

TOASTED OATMEAL BREAD
Mrs. Wallace Anderson, Colon, Nebraska

I entered this special bread recipe in our state fair, and it won a blue ribbon. It's been a holiday favorite of mine ever since!

6 to 6-1/2 cups all-purpose flour, *divided*
1/4 cup sugar
2 packages (1/4 ounce *each*) active dry yeast
1-1/2 teaspoons salt
1-1/3 cups water
1/4 cup milk
1/4 cup molasses
1/4 cup butter *or* margarine
1 egg
1 cup old-fashioned oats, lightly toasted
2-1/2 cups chopped walnuts

In a mixing bowl, combine 1 cup flour, sugar, yeast and salt; mix well. In a small saucepan, heat water, milk, molasses and butter until a thermometer reads 120°-130° (butter does not need to melt). Add to yeast mixture; beat on medium speed for 2 minutes. Add egg, oats and 2 cups flour; beat on high for 2 minutes. Stir in nuts and enough remaining flour to form a soft dough. Turn onto a floured board; knead until smooth and elastic, 6-8 minutes. Place in a greased bowl, turning once to grease top. Cover and let rise in a warm place until doubled, about 1-1/2 hours. Punch dough down. Shape into two round loaves; place on greased baking sheets. With a sharp knife, cut four parallel slashes on top of each loaf. Cover and let rise until doubled, about 1 hour. Bake at 375° for 20-30 minutes or until golden brown. Remove from pans; cool on wire racks. **Yield:** 2 loaves.

BLUEBERRY-ORANGE COFFEE CAKE
Kathy Fannoun, Robbinsdale, Minnesota

The orange peel and fresh juice in this cake give it a delicious aroma and a moist texture, while the blueberries add color.

5 cups all-purpose flour
1 cup sugar
3/4 cup packed brown sugar, *divided*
2 tablespoons baking powder
1/2 teaspoon salt
2 to 3 teaspoons grated orange peel
3/4 cup butter *or* margarine
1 cup chopped walnuts
2 eggs plus 2 egg whites
2 cups milk
1 tablespoon orange juice
2 teaspoons vanilla extract
2-1/2 cups fresh *or* frozen blueberries
1-1/2 teaspoons ground cinnamon

In a bowl, combine flour, sugar, 1/2 cup brown sugar, baking powder, salt and orange peel. Cut in butter until mixture resembles coarse crumbs. Add nuts. Beat eggs, whites, milk, juice and vanilla; stir into dry ingredients just until moistened. Fold in berries. Spoon half into a greased 10-in. fluted tube pan. Combine cinnamon and remaining brown sugar; sprinkle over batter. Top with remaining batter. Bake at 350° for 1 hour and 20 minutes or until a wooden pick inserted near the center comes out clean. Cool in pan 10 minutes. Invert onto a serving plate. **Yield:** 16-20 servings.

SWEET RYE BREAD
Dee Hendershot, Parkers Prairie, Minnesota

This bread has a slightly sweet flavor for a nice change of pace from the traditional rye. It's also wonderful toasted.

2 packages (1/4 ounce *each*) active dry yeast
3-1/3 cups warm water (110° to 115°), *divided*
1/2 cup evaporated milk
1/2 cup butter *or* margarine, melted
2/3 cup packed brown sugar
1/2 cup dark corn syrup
3 tablespoons molasses
1-1/2 teaspoons salt
3 cups rye flour
9 to 10 cups all-purpose flour
Melted butter or margarine

In a large mixing bowl, dissolve yeast in 2 cups water; let stand for 15 minutes. Add milk, butter, sugar, corn syrup, molasses, salt and remaining water. Stir in rye flour. Gradually add enough all-purpose flour to form a soft dough. Turn onto a lightly floured board; knead until smooth and elastic, 6-8 minutes. Place in a greased bowl, turning once to grease top. Cover and let rise in a warm place until doubled, about 1 hour. Punch dough down. Shape into four loaves; place in greased 8-in. x 4-in. x 2-in. loaf pans. Cover and let rise until doubled, about 1 hour. Bake at 325° for 40-45 minutes. Remove from pans to cool on wire racks. Brush with melted butter. **Yield:** 4 loaves.

CORNMEAL YEAST BREAD
Edith Pelon, Fife Lake, Michigan

Every time I take this unique bread to a potluck, I get lots of requests for the recipe. It's also tasty in a stuffing.

7-1/4 to 7-3/4 cups all-purpose flour, *divided*
1 cup yellow cornmeal
2 packages (1/4 ounce *each*) active dry yeast
2 cups milk
1/2 cup butter *or* margarine
1/2 cup sugar
1-1/2 teaspoons salt
2 eggs
Melted butter *or* margarine

In a mixing bowl, combine 3 cups of flour, cornmeal and yeast. In a small saucepan, heat milk, butter, sugar and salt until a thermometer reaches 120°-130° (butter does not need to melt). Blend into yeast mixture on low just until moistened. Add eggs; beat on low for 30 seconds. Beat on high for 3 minutes. Stir in enough remaining flour to form a stiff dough. Turn onto a floured board; knead until smooth and elastic, 6-8 minutes. Place in a greased bowl, turning once to grease top. Cover and let rise in a warm place until doubled, about 1-1/4 hours. Punch dough down; knead four to five times. Shape into two loaves and place in greased 8-in. x 4-in. x 2-in. loaf pans. Cover and let rise until doubled, about 30 minutes. Brush with butter. Bake at 375° for 30 minutes. Remove from pans to cool on wire racks. **Yield:** 2 loaves.

Appetizers

A special beverage and tempting finger foods can set the stage for any holiday get-together.

CRANBERRY TEA
Kathy Traetow, Waverly, Iowa
(Pictured on page 19)

This colorful tea with its sweet spicy flavor is a great winter warmer-upper. The aroma is sure to bring guests to the table!

  1 bottle (32 ounces) cranberry juice
  2 cups sugar
  1 can (6 ounces) frozen orange juice concentrate
  1 can (6 ounces) frozen lemonade concentrate
1/3 cup red-hot candies
  1 cinnamon stick
  2 whole cloves

In a 3-qt. saucepan, combine all ingredients; bring to a boil over medium heat. Boil for 7 minutes, stirring occasionally. Remove cinnamon and cloves. To serve, mix 1 cup concentrate and 2 cups water; heat through. Store concentrate in a covered container in the refrigerator. **Yield:** 18 cups (1-1/2 quarts concentrate).

DILL VEGETABLE DIP
Karen Gardiner, Eutaw, Alabama
(Pictured on page 19)

A friend gave me this zesty dip recipe many years ago, and now I serve it every year at our holiday open house.

  1 cup (8 ounces) sour cream
1/2 cup mayonnaise
  1 tablespoon finely chopped onion
  2 teaspoons dried parsley flakes
  1 teaspoon dill weed
  1 teaspoon seasoned salt
Assorted fresh vegetables

Combine the first six ingredients; mix well. Cover and refrigerate. Serve with vegetables. **Yield:** 1-1/2 cups.

MUSHROOM CRESCENTS
Mavis Diment, Marcus, Iowa
(Pictured on page 19)

These tasty appetizers are popular at holiday parties. They can be prepared ahead and reheated.

  1 package (8 ounces) cream cheese, softened
1/2 cup butter *or* margarine, softened
1-1/2 cups all-purpose flour
FILLING:
1/2 pound fresh mushrooms, finely chopped
  1 medium onion, finely chopped
  2 tablespoons butter *or* margarine
  1 package (3 ounces) cream cheese, cubed
1/2 teaspoon salt
1/4 teaspoon dried thyme

1/8 teaspoon pepper
  1 egg, lightly beaten
  1 teaspoon water

In a mixing bowl, beat cream cheese and butter until smooth; stir in flour. Cover and refrigerate dough for at least 1 hour. Meanwhile, in a skillet or saucepan over medium heat, saute mushrooms and onion in butter until tender. Remove from the heat. Add cream cheese, salt, thyme and pepper; stir until cheese is melted. Cool to room temperature. On a floured surface, roll dough to 1/8-in. thickness. Cut into 3-in. circles. Combine egg and water; lightly brush edges of circles. Place about 1 teaspoon of filling in center of each circle. Fold over; seal edges. Brush with egg mixture. Bake at 400° for 15-20 minutes or until golden brown. **Yield:** about 4 dozen.

PINEAPPLE SMOKIES
Dorothy Anderson, Ottawa, Kansas
(Pictured on page 19)

These sausages in a tangy-sweet sauce make an excellent holiday snack. The recipe is quick and easy but makes lots.

  1 cup packed brown sugar
  3 tablespoons all-purpose flour
  2 teaspoons ground mustard
  1 cup pineapple juice
1/2 cup vinegar
1-1/2 teaspoons soy sauce
  2 pounds mini smoked sausage links

In a large saucepan, combine sugar, flour and mustard. Gradually stir in pineapple juice, vinegar and soy sauce. Bring to a boil over medium heat, stirring occasionally. Boil for 2 minutes, stirring constantly. Add sausages; stir to coat. Cook for 5 minutes or until heated through. Serve warm. **Yield:** about 8 dozen.

BACON CHEESE SPREAD
Sharon Bickett, Chester, South Carolina
(Pictured on page 19)

Each year, I share Christmas cheer by setting up a buffet at my family's hardware store. This spread is always a hit!

  1 package (12 ounces) bacon strips, chopped
1/2 cup chopped pecans *or* almonds, toasted
  4 cups (1 pound) shredded sharp cheddar cheese
  2 cups mayonnaise
  1 small onion, chopped
  2 tablespoons finely chopped sweet red pepper
1/8 teaspoon cayenne pepper
Assorted crackers

Cook bacon until crisp; drain. Mix with the next six ingredients. Serve with crackers. **Yield:** 4 cups.

APPEALING APPETIZERS. Starting clockwise from the top: Pineapple Smokies, Cranberry Tea, Bacon Cheese Spread, Mushroom Crescents, Dill Vegetable Dip. Recipes are on p. 18.

Christmas Dinner

With these recipes, you'll prepare a festive feast sure to please everyone around the table!

HONEY-GLAZED TURKEY
Mary Smolka, Spring Grove, Illinois
(Pictured on page 22)

Even during the holidays, my husband wouldn't eat turkey ...until I tried this recipe. Now, he loves it! The sweet and spicy glaze gives the turkey a wonderful flavor.

       2 cups chopped onion
1-1/2 cups chopped celery
   1/2 cup butter *or* margarine
    12 cups unseasoned stuffing croutons *or* dry bread cubes
     1 tablespoon poultry seasoning
     2 teaspoons chicken bouillon granules
     1 teaspoon pepper
     1 teaspoon dried rosemary, crushed
     1 teaspoon lemon-pepper seasoning
   1/2 teaspoon salt
     2 to 2-1/2 cups boiling water
     1 turkey (14 to 16 pounds)
GLAZE:
   1/2 cup honey
   1/2 cup Dijon mustard
1-1/2 teaspoons dried rosemary, crushed
     1 teaspoon onion powder
   1/2 teaspoon salt
   1/4 teaspoon garlic powder
   1/4 teaspoon pepper

In a large skillet, saute onion and celery in butter until tender. Pour into a large bowl. Add the next seven ingredients; mix well. Stir in enough water until stuffing has reached desired moistness. Just before baking, stuff the turkey. Skewer openings; tie drumsticks together. Place on a rack in a roasting pan. Cover lightly with a tent of aluminum foil. Bake at 325° for 4 hours. Combine glaze ingredients. Pour over turkey. Bake an additional 1 to 1-1/2 hours, basting if needed, or until a meat thermometer reads 185°. Remove all stuffing. If desired, thicken drippings for gravy. **Yield:** 12-14 servings (about 12 cups stuffing). **Editor's Note:** Stuffing may be baked in a greased 3-qt. covered baking dish at 325° for 70 minutes (uncover the last 10 minutes). Turkey may also be prepared in an oven roasting bag. Pour glaze over stuffed turkey and bake according to package directions.

BROCCOLI ELEGANT
Carolyn Griffin, Macon, Georgia
(Pictured on page 22)

My family loves this creamy vegetable side dish. As pretty as it is tasty, it's an extra-special way to serve broccoli, and it really dresses up a table.

     3 cups water
   1/2 cup plus 2 tablespoons butter *or* margarine, *divided*

     2 boxes (6 ounces *each*) corn bread stuffing mix
     2 packages (10 ounces *each*) frozen broccoli spears, cooked and drained
     2 tablespoons all-purpose flour
   1/2 teaspoon chicken bouillon granules
   1/4 teaspoon salt
1-1/3 cups milk
     1 package (3 ounces) cream cheese, softened and cubed
     2 green onions, sliced
   1/2 cup shredded cheddar cheese
   1/8 teaspoon paprika

In a saucepan over medium heat, combine water, 1/4 cup butter and seasoning packet from stuffing mixes; bring to a boil. Remove from the heat; add stuffing crumbs and toss. Let stand 5 minutes. Spoon stuffing around edges of a greased 13-in. x 9-in. x 2-in. baking dish. Place broccoli spears in center of dish. In a saucepan over medium heat, melt remaining butter. Add flour, bouillon and salt; stir to form a smooth paste. Gradually add milk, stirring constantly; bring to a boil. Cook and stir for 2 minutes or until thickened. Add cream cheese; stir until melted. Add onions; mix well. Pour over center of broccoli. Cover and bake at 350° for 20-25 minutes or until heated through. Sprinkle with cheese and paprika. **Yield:** 8-10 servings.

CHRISTMAS SALAD
Jan Renaud, Lisle, Illinois
(Pictured on pages 22-23)

I enjoy entertaining during the holidays and always include this colorful salad on the menu. The red pepper and water chestnuts add a sweet crunch...while the homemade vinaigrette gives this salad a savory zest.

CRANBERRY VINAIGRETTE:
   1/4 cup white wine vinegar
   1/2 cup fresh *or* frozen cranberries, thawed
     2 green onions, cut into 1-inch pieces
     1 tablespoon sugar
1-1/2 teaspoons Dijon mustard
   1/2 teaspoon salt
   1/4 teaspoon pepper
   1/4 teaspoon dried sage, crushed
   3/4 cup olive *or* vegetable oil
SALAD:
    12 cups mixed greens
     1 small sweet red pepper, chopped
     1 can (8 ounces) sliced water chestnuts, drained, optional
Grated *or* shredded Parmesan cheese, optional

In a blender, combine the first eight ingredients. With the blender on high speed, gradually add the oil through the cap opening; process until smooth. Chill until ready to serve. In a large salad bowl, combine greens, red pepper and water chestnuts if desired. Sprinkle with Parmesan if desired. Serve with cranberry vinaigrette. **Yield:** 12 servings (1 cup vinaigrette).

SPICED HOLIDAY HAM
Eunice Hurt, Murfreesboro, Tennessee
(Pictured on page 23)

This glazed ham is one of my family's favorites, so I serve it often at holiday time. Currant jelly, mustard and brown sugar add a special flavor.

    1 bone-in half ham (5 to 7 pounds)
   15 whole cloves
    1 jar (12 ounces) currant jelly
    1 tablespoon brown sugar
    1 tablespoon vinegar
    1 teaspoon ground mustard
  1/4 teaspoon ground cinnamon

Score ham; insert cloves in cuts. Place in a greased 13-in. x 9-in. x 2-in. baking dish. Bake, uncovered, at 325° for 20 minutes *per pound*. Combine jelly, sugar, vinegar, mustard and cinnamon; brush half over ham. Bake 15 minutes. Brush remaining jelly mixture over ham. Bake for 15 minutes, basting occasionally, or until a meat thermometer reads 140°. **Yield:** 8-10 servings.

ENGLISH BATTER BUNS
Geraldine West, Ogden, Utah
(Pictured on page 22)

Since receiving this easy-to-prepare recipe from a dear friend, I've made these rolls often for the holidays.

    2 packages (1/4 ounce *each*) active dry yeast
    1 cup warm milk (110° to 115°)
  1/2 cup shortening
    2 tablespoons sugar
    1 teaspoon salt
    2 eggs, beaten
3-1/2 cups all-purpose flour
Butter *or* margarine, melted

In a large mixing bowl, dissolve yeast in milk. Add shortening, sugar, salt, eggs and 2 cups of flour; beat 2 minutes. Stir in remaining flour until smooth. Cover and let rise in a warm place until doubled, about 30 minutes. Stir batter vigorously for 25 strokes (dough will be slightly sticky). Spoon into 12 greased muffin cups. Tap pans to settle the batter. Cover and let rise until batter reaches tops of cups, about 20 minutes. Bake at 400° for 10-15 minutes or until golden brown. Brush with butter. **Yield:** 1 dozen.

CRANBERRY-ORANGE RELISH
Vonna Wendt, Ephrata, Washington
(Pictured on pages 22-23)

I always include this delicious fruity relish as part of our special Christmas Eve dinner.

    1 unpeeled navel orange
    2 cups fresh *or* frozen cranberries
    1 unpeeled medium red apple
    1 package (3 ounces) raspberry gelatin
1-1/3 cups boiling water
    1 can (20 ounces) crushed pineapple, undrained
  1/2 cup chopped walnuts

Slice the orange into eighths; finely chop in a food processor. Add cranberries and process until chopped. Slice apple into eighths; add to orange mixture and process until chopped. In a large bowl, dissolve gelatin in boiling water; stir in pineapple and orange mixture. Chill for at least 4 hours. Just before serving, stir in nuts. **Yield:** 12 servings.

CHOCOLATE PEPPERMINT CAKE
Jeanne Bloedorn, Fond du Lac, Wisconsin
(Pictured on page 23)

Guests make sure to save room for this light and moist cake with its refreshing mint flavor and chocolate glaze. Its seasonal look makes it perfect for Christmas...a holiday birthday party...or other festive gatherings!

    2 cups sugar
1-3/4 cups all-purpose flour
  3/4 cup baking cocoa
1-1/2 teaspoons baking soda
1-1/2 teaspoons baking powder
    1 teaspoon salt
    1 cup milk
  1/2 cup vegetable oil
    2 eggs
    2 teaspoons vanilla extract
    1 cup boiling water
FILLING:
    2 cups whipping cream
  1/4 cup confectioners' sugar
    1 teaspoon vanilla extract
    2 drops red food coloring, optional
  2/3 cup crushed peppermint candy, *divided*
GLAZE:
    2 tablespoons butter *or* margarine
    2 tablespoons baking cocoa
    2 tablespoons water
  1/2 teaspoon vanilla extract
    1 cup confectioners' sugar

In a mixing bowl, combine dry ingredients. Add milk, oil, eggs and vanilla; beat at medium speed for 2 minutes. Stir in boiling water (batter will be thin). Pour into three greased and floured 9-in. round baking pans. Bake at 350° for 18-23 minutes or until cake tests done. Cool in pan 10 minutes; remove to a wire rack to cool completely. For filling, beat cream until soft peaks form. Add sugar, vanilla and food coloring if desired; beat until stiff peaks form. Set aside about 1 tablespoon crushed candy. Fold remaining candy into cream mixture. Spread between layers and around sides but not over the top. For glaze, melt butter in a saucepan over low heat. Add cocoa and water; cook, stirring constantly, until slightly thickened. Remove from the heat; whisk in vanilla. Gradually blend in sugar until smooth. Add additional water if necessary. Spread on top of cake. Sprinkle reserved candy over glaze. Chill before serving. Store in the refrigerator. **Yield:** 12-16 servings.

FEAST FOR THE EYES! Clockwise from top right: Chocolate Peppermint Cake (p. 21), Spiced Holiday Ham (p. 21), Cherry Date Fruitcake (p. 24), Cranberry-Orange Relish (p. 21), Broccoli Elegant (p. 20), English Batter Buns (p. 21), Honey-Glazed Turkey (p. 20), Christmas Salad (p. 20).

CHERRY DATE FRUITCAKE
Judy Schultz, Jamestown, New York
(Pictured on page 23)

It's a Christmas tradition for me to serve this fruitcake at parties and to give it to friends and family. Jam-packed with nuts and cherries, it puts a new spin on a holiday mainstay.

1-1/2 cups all-purpose flour
1-1/2 cups sugar
   1 teaspoon baking powder
   1 teaspoon salt
5-1/2 cups pecan halves
   2 jars (16 ounces *each*) maraschino cherries, drained and halved
   1 pound diced candied pineapple
   2 packages (8 ounces *each*) chopped pitted dates
   6 eggs
   1/2 cup apple juice
   1/4 cup light corn syrup

In a large bowl, combine the first four ingredients. Add pecans, cherries, pineapple and dates; toss to coat. Beat eggs and apple juice; add to fruit mixture and mix well. Grease two foil-lined 9-in. x 5-in. x 3-in. loaf pans. Press half of the mixture into each pan. Bake at 300° for 1-3/4 to 2 hours or until a wooden pick inserted near the center comes out clean. Cool in pans on a wire rack for 10 minutes. Remove from pans and remove foil. Brush each loaf with corn syrup. Cool completely. **Yield:** 2 fruitcakes.

WHOLE WHEAT BUTTERHORNS
Mildred Sherrer, Bay City, Texas

These delicious whole wheat rolls go well with all types of dinner entrees. Be prepared, though! Their tempting buttery flavor is sure to have your guests asking for seconds.

2-1/4 to 2-3/4 cups all-purpose flour, *divided*
   2 packages (1/4 ounce *each*) active dry yeast
1-1/2 cups water
   1/3 cup packed brown sugar
   2 tablespoons honey
   2 teaspoons salt
   5 tablespoons butter *or* margarine, *divided*
   2 cups whole wheat flour

In a large mixing bowl, combine 1-1/2 cups all-purpose flour and yeast. In a small saucepan, heat water, brown sugar, honey, salt and 3 tablespoons butter until a thermometer reaches 120°-130° (butter does not need to melt). Add to yeast mixture; beat on low for 30 seconds. Beat on high for 3 minutes. Stir in whole wheat flour and enough remaining all-purpose flour to form a soft dough. Turn onto a floured board; knead until smooth and elastic, 6-8 minutes. Place in a greased bowl, turning once to grease top. Cover and let rise in a warm place until doubled, about 1-1/2 hours. Punch dough down and divide into thirds. Shape each portion into a ball; cover and let rest for 10 minutes. On a lightly floured board, roll each ball into a 12-in. circle. Cut each circle into six to eight pie-shaped wedges. Beginning at the wide end, roll up each wedge. Place rolls, point side down, 2 in. apart on greased baking sheets. Cover and let rise until doubled, about 1 hour. Melt remaining butter; brush over rolls.

Bake at 400° for 10-15 minutes or until golden brown. Immediately remove from pans; cool on wire racks. **Yield:** 1-1/2 to 2 dozen.

FANCY BRUSSELS SPROUTS
Lucy Meyring, Walden, Colorado

Here's a great way to dress up brussels sprouts. Almonds give this rich creamy dish a nutty texture and flavor.

1-1/4 pounds fresh brussels sprouts *or* 1 package (18 ounces) frozen brussels sprouts
   1 can (10-3/4 ounces) condensed cream of mushroom soup, undiluted
   1/4 cup milk
   1 cup (4 ounces) shredded sharp cheddar cheese
   1/8 teaspoon salt
   1/8 teaspoon pepper
   1 can (8 ounces) sliced water chestnuts, drained
   1/2 cup slivered almonds, toasted

Cook brussels sprouts in boiling water. Meanwhile, in a saucepan over medium heat, combine the soup, milk, cheese, salt and pepper; cook and stir until cheese melts. Drain brussels sprouts; transfer to a serving dish. Add water chestnuts and cheese sauce. Sprinkle with almonds. Serve immediately. **Yield:** 6-8 servings.

NUTTY SWEET POTATO BAKE
Dorothy Pritchett, Wills Point, Texas

Even people who say they don't like traditional sweet potato dishes come back for more of this yummy casserole.

   4 eggs
   1 cup sugar
   1 cup milk
   1/4 cup butter *or* margarine, melted
   6 cups cubed cooked sweet potatoes *or* 2 cans (40 ounces *each*) cut yams, drained
TOPPING:
   1 cup all-purpose flour
   1 cup packed brown sugar
   1/2 cup butter *or* margarine, melted
   1 cup chopped pecans

In a large bowl, beat eggs. Add sugar, milk and butter; mix well. Add sweet potatoes and mix gently. Pour into a greased 13-in. x 9-in. x 2-in. baking dish. For topping, combine flour and sugar in a small bowl. Stir in butter and pecans; mix well. Sprinkle over sweet potatoes. Bake, uncovered, at 350° for 55-65 minutes or until a knife inserted near the center comes out clean. **Yield:** 16 servings.

PECAN-CORN BREAD DRESSING
***Country Woman* Test Kitchen**

Plenty of pecans and bacon give this stuffing a unique flavor—while using a packaged mix cuts down on the preparation time.

   3 cups water
   1/2 cup butter *or* margarine

1 package (16 ounces) corn bread stuffing mix
10 bacon strips, diced
1 cup chopped celery
1-1/2 cups chopped green onions
1/2 cup coarsely chopped pecans
1/2 teaspoon salt
1/4 teaspoon pepper

In a large saucepan, bring water and butter to a boil. Remove from the heat and stir in stuffing mix; cover and set aside. In a large skillet, cook bacon until crisp; remove with a slotted spoon to drain on paper towels. Discard all but 3 tablespoons of drippings; cook celery in drippings over medium heat for 5 minutes. Add onions and cook 5 minutes or until celery is tender, stirring constantly. Add to corn bread mixture along with pecans, salt, pepper and bacon; mix well. Pour into a greased 2-qt. casserole. Cover and bake at 325° for 45 minutes. **Yield:** 8 cups.

CREAMY CHEESE SOUP
Jan Campbell, Purvis, Mississippi

We have a large family, so I always plan a big holiday menu. This time-saving first course is enjoyed by everyone—including the cook!

1/3 cup *each* chopped carrots, celery and green
    onions
1/2 cup water
1 cup chopped onion
1/2 cup butter *or* margarine
3/4 cup all-purpose flour
4 cups milk
3 cups chicken broth
1 jar (16 ounces) process cheese sauce
1/8 teaspoon cayenne pepper

In a saucepan, bring carrots, celery, green onions and water to a boil; reduce heat. Simmer until crisp-tender; drain. Place in a blender or food processor; puree until smooth. In a 3-qt. saucepan over medium heat, saute onion in butter. Add flour; stir to form a smooth paste. Gradually add milk and broth, stirring constantly; bring to a boil. Cook and stir 2 minutes or until thickened; reduce heat. Add cheese sauce, cayenne and pureed vegetables. Stir until cheese is melted. **Yield:** 8-10 servings (2-1/2 quarts).

AMBROSIA PECAN PIE
Bernadine Stine, Roanoke, Indiana

Orange peel and coconut combine with pecans to make this truly special and rich-tasting dessert. It always wins compliments at Christmas dinner.

3 eggs
3/4 cup light corn syrup
1/2 cup sugar
3 tablespoons brown sugar
3 tablespoons orange juice
2 tablespoons butter *or* margarine, melted
1 teaspoon grated orange peel
1/8 teaspoon salt
1-1/2 cups chopped pecans

2/3 cup flaked coconut
1 unbaked pastry shell (9 inches)

In a large mixing bowl, beat eggs, corn syrup, sugars, orange juice, butter, orange peel and salt until well blended. Stir in pecans and coconut. Pour into pastry shell. Bake at 350° for 50-60 minutes or until a knife inserted near the center comes out clean. If edges become too brown, cover with foil. Cool on a wire rack. **Yield:** 8 servings.

FESTIVE CAULIFLOWER CASSEROLE
Nancy McDonald, Burns, Wyoming

My family asks for this dish every Christmas. It complements turkey or ham…and can be put together the day before the meal—a real convenience for a cook when the holiday rush is in full swing.

1 large head cauliflower (2 pounds), cut into florets
1/4 cup diced green pepper
1 jar (4-1/2 ounces) sliced mushrooms, drained
1/4 cup butter *or* margarine
1/3 cup all-purpose flour
3/4 teaspoon salt
2 cups milk
1 jar (2 ounces) diced pimientos, drained
1 cup (4 ounces) shredded Swiss cheese, *divided*

Cook cauliflower in boiling salted water until crisp-tender; drain. Place in a greased 8-in. square baking dish. In a saucepan over medium heat, saute green pepper and mushrooms in butter until tender. Add flour and salt; stir to form a smooth paste. Gradually add milk; bring to a boil, stirring constantly. Cook and stir 2 minutes more or until thickened. Remove from the heat; add pimientos. Stir in 3/4 cup cheese until melted; pour over cauliflower. Cover and bake at 350° for 20 minutes. Sprinkle with remaining cheese; return to the oven, uncovered, for 10-15 minutes or until cheese is melted. **Yield:** 6-8 servings.

CRANBERRY MOUSSE SALAD
Sue Warner, Garner, North Carolina

My sister and I discovered this recipe while looking for something different to serve at holiday time. The fruity flavor goes especially well with poultry or pork.

1 package (6 ounces) strawberry gelatin
3/4 cup boiling water
1 can (16 ounces) whole-berry cranberry sauce
2 tablespoons fresh lemon juice
1 teaspoon grated lemon peel
1/4 teaspoon ground nutmeg
1 can (20 ounces) crushed pineapple
2 cups (16 ounces) sour cream
1/2 cup chopped pecans

In a bowl, dissolve gelatin in water. Add cranberry sauce, lemon juice, peel and nutmeg; mix well. Drain pineapple; add juice to gelatin mixture and set pineapple aside. Chill until syrupy. Whisk in sour cream. Add the pineapple and pecans. Pour into an oiled 8-cup mold. Chill until firm. **Yield:** 10-12 servings.

 # Holiday Cookies

Make the season sweeter for family, friends—even Santa himself—with this selection of Christmas cookies.

MACAROON KISSES
Alice McTarnaghan, Castleton, New York
(Pictured on page 28)

These cookies are a holiday favorite around our house. You can top them off with cherries or chocolate—or some of each!

      1/3 cup butter *or* margarine, softened
        1 package (3 ounces) cream cheese, softened
      3/4 cup sugar
        1 egg yolk
    1-1/2 teaspoons almond extract
        2 teaspoons orange juice
    1-1/4 cups all-purpose flour
        2 teaspoons baking powder
      1/4 teaspoon salt
        5 cups coconut, *divided*
    Candied cherries *and/or* chocolate kisses

In a mixing bowl, cream butter, cream cheese and sugar until light and fluffy. Combine egg yolk, extract and juice; add to creamed mixture and mix well. Combine flour, baking powder and salt; gradually add to creamed mixture and mix well. Stir in 3 cups of coconut. Cover and chill for at least 1 hour. Shape into 1-in. balls; roll in remaining coconut. Place 2 in. apart on ungreased baking sheets. Bake at 350° for 10-12 minutes or until lightly browned. Immediately place a cherry or chocolate kiss on top of each cookie. Cool 5 minutes; remove to a wire rack to cool completely. **Yield:** about 4 dozen.

PECAN HORNS
Dolores Gruenewald, Grove, Oklahoma
(Pictured on pages 28-29)

These cookies have a nutty, slightly sweet taste. They go well served with coffee or tea at festive get-togethers.

        2 cups all-purpose flour
    1-1/2 tablespoons sugar
      1/2 teaspoon salt
        1 cup butter *or* margarine
        1 egg plus 1 egg yolk
        1 teaspoon vanilla extract
    FILLING/TOPPING:
    1-1/2 cups ground pecans, *divided*
      1/2 cup sugar, *divided*
      1/4 teaspoon grated lemon peel
      1/4 cup milk
        1 egg white, beaten

In a mixing bowl, combine flour, sugar and salt. Cut in butter until mixture resembles coarse crumbs. Combine egg, yolk and vanilla; add to flour mixture. Mix well and form into a ball. Chill about 1 hour or until firm enough to handle. Meanwhile, for filling, combine 1-1/4 cups pecans, 1/4 cup sugar, lemon peel and milk; set aside. Cut

dough into four sections; shape 12 balls out of each section. Flatten each ball into a 2-1/2-in. round; top with a scant teaspoon of filling. Fold dough over filling; seal and shape like a horn. Place on ungreased baking sheets. Combine remaining pecans and sugar. Brush egg white over horns; sprinkle with pecan mixture. Bake at 350° for 25 minutes or until lightly browned. **Yield:** 4 dozen.

ROLL-OUT COOKIES
Bonnie Price, Yelm, Washington
(Pictured on page 28)

I collect cookie cutters (I have over 5,000!), so a good cutout recipe is a must. These cookies are crisp and buttery-tasting with just a hint of lemon, and the dough handles nicely.

        1 cup butter *or* margarine, softened
        1 cup sugar
        1 egg
        1 teaspoon vanilla extract
      1/2 teaspoon lemon extract
        3 cups all-purpose flour
        2 teaspoons baking powder
    GLAZE:
        1 cup confectioners' sugar
        2 tablespoons water
        1 tablespoon light corn syrup
    Food coloring, optional

In a mixing bowl, cream butter and sugar. Add egg and extracts. Combine flour and baking powder; gradually add to creamed mixture and mix well. (Dough will be very stiff. If necessary, stir in the last cup of flour mixture by hand. Do not chill.) On a lightly floured surface, roll dough to 1/8-in. thickness. Cut out cookies into desired shapes. Place 2 in. apart on ungreased baking sheets. Bake at 400° for 6-7 minutes or until edges are lightly browned. Cool 2 minutes before removing to wire racks; cool completely. For glaze, combine the sugar, water and corn syrup until smooth. Tint with food coloring if desired. Using a small brush and stirring glaze often, brush on cookies, decorating as desired. **Yield:** about 6 dozen (2-1/4-inch cookies).

SPLIT-SECOND COOKIES
Mrs. Richard Foust, Stoneboro, Pennsylvania
(Pictured on page 28)

I love baking cookies, and this is a recipe I've used for many Christmases over the years. Raspberry jam makes these cookies flavorful and colorful.

      3/4 cup butter *or* margarine, softened
      2/3 cup sugar
        1 egg
        1 teaspoon vanilla extract
        2 cups all-purpose flour

1/2 teaspoon baking powder
1/2 teaspoon salt
1/3 cup raspberry jam

In a mixing bowl, cream butter and sugar. Add egg and vanilla; mix well. Combine flour, baking powder and salt; gradually add to creamed mixture and mix well. Divide dough into four equal portions; shape each into a 12-in. x 3/4-in. log. Place 4 in. apart on greased baking sheets. Make a 1/2-in. depression down center of logs; fill with jam. Bake at 350° for 15-20 minutes or until lightly browned. Cool for 2 minutes; cut diagonally into 3/4-in. slices. Remove to wire racks to cool completely. **Yield:** about 5 dozen.

ITALIAN HOLIDAY COOKIES
Sue Seymour, Valatie, New York
(Pictured on page 29)

Many of our holiday traditions center around the foods my mother made while I was growing up. These cookies, which we called "Strufoli", bring back wonderful memories.

    1 tablespoon sugar
    1 teaspoon grated lemon peel
    1 teaspoon vanilla extract
    1/2 teaspoon salt
    4 eggs
2-1/2 cups all-purpose flour
Cooking oil for deep-fat frying
    1 cup honey
Candy sprinkles

In a mixing bowl, combine sugar, lemon peel, vanilla and salt. Add eggs and 2 cups flour; mix well. Turn onto a floured board and knead in remaining flour (dough will be soft). With a floured knife or scissors, cut into 20 pieces. With hands, roll each piece into pencil shapes. Cut "pencils" into 1/2-in. pieces. In an electric skillet or deep-fat fryer, heat oil to 350°. Fry pieces, a few at a time, for 2 minutes per side or until golden brown. Drain on paper towels. Place in a large bowl. Heat honey to boiling; pour over cookies and mix well. With a slotted spoon, spoon onto a serving platter and slowly mound into a tree shape if desired. Decorate with candy sprinkles. Cool completely. **Yield:** about 15 dozen.

CHRISTMAS CANDY COOKIES
Joan Graham, Angel Fire, New Mexico
(Pictured on page 29)

These delightful cookies hold up well in care packages I send to friends and relatives. They're also the first to go at potlucks when people come back to the table for one more sweet treat.

    1 cup butter *or* margarine, softened
    1 cup sugar
    1 cup confectioners' sugar
    1 cup vegetable oil
    2 eggs
    1 teaspoon almond extract
3-1/2 cups all-purpose flour
    1 cup whole wheat flour
    1 teaspoon baking soda

    1 teaspoon salt
    1 teaspoon cream of tartar
    1 cup chopped almonds
    1 package (8 ounces) mini red and green M&M's
      or Heath baking bits
Additional sugar

In a mixing bowl, cream butter, sugars and oil. Add eggs and extract; mix well. Combine flours, baking soda, salt and cream of tartar; gradually add to creamed mixture and mix well. Stir in almonds and candy. Chill for 1 hour or until firm enough to handle. Shape into 1-in. balls; roll in sugar. Place on ungreased baking sheets. Flatten with a flat-bottomed glass. Bake at 350° for 15-18 minutes or until lightly browned. Cool on wire racks. **Yield:** about 8 dozen.

REINDEER COOKIES
Flo Burtnett, Gage, Oklahoma
(Pictured below)

This is one cookie recipe I especially enjoy making. My grandchildren love the graham cracker taste and the cute reindeer shape. I like that they're so quick and easy to assemble!

    1 cup confectioners' sugar
    1 teaspoon vanilla extract
    3 to 4 tablespoons whipping cream
    12 graham cracker halves
    24 chocolate chips
    12 red-hot candies
    12 mini pretzel twists

In a small bowl, combine sugar, vanilla and enough cream to reach a spreading consistency; cover and set aside. Using a serrated knife and a gentle sawing motion, cut graham crackers diagonally in half, forming two triangles. Frost one triangle. With frosted triangle on bottom, overlap triangles so the shortest side of unfrosted triangle runs along the longest cut edge of frosted triangle; match smallest points of crackers to form the nose. The remaining narrow points of both crackers form the ears (see photo below). Frost top cracker. Gently press on chocolate chips for eyes and a red-hot for nose. Using the serrated knife and a gentle sawing motion, cut pretzels in half to form antlers; press onto ears. Place on wire rack until set. **Yield:** 1 dozen. **Editor's Note:** It is a good idea to have a few extra graham crackers and pretzels on hand because they break easily when cut.

CHRISTMAS COOKIE CREATIONS. Clockwise from top right: Christmas Candy Cookies (p. 27), Strawberry Oatmeal Bars (p. 30), Roll-Out Cookies (p. 26), Split-Second Cookies (p. 26), Macaroon Kisses (p. 26), Italian Holiday Cookies (p. 27), Pecan Horns, center (p. 26).

STRAWBERRY OATMEAL BARS
Flo Burtnett, Gage, Oklahoma
(Pictured on page 29)

Their fruity filling and fluffy coconut topping make these bars truly one of a kind. They really dress up my trays of Christmas goodies.

1-1/4 cups all-purpose flour
1-1/4 cups quick-cooking oats
  1/2 cup sugar
  1/2 teaspoon baking powder
  1/4 teaspoon salt
  3/4 cup butter *or* margarine, melted
   2 teaspoons vanilla extract
   1 cup strawberry preserves
  1/2 cup flaked coconut

In a bowl, combine dry ingredients. Add butter and vanilla; stir until crumbly. Set aside 1 cup. Press remaining crumb mixture evenly into an ungreased 13-in. x 9-in. x 2-in. baking pan. Spread preserves over crust. Combine coconut and reserved crumb mixture; sprinkle over preserves. Bake at 350° for 25-30 minutes or until coconut is lightly browned. Cool. **Yield:** 3 dozen.

OATMEAL GINGERSNAPS
Sherry Harke, South Bend, Indiana

I always get compliments on these delicious chewy cookies. The spicy aroma fills my kitchen when they're baking and never fails to set a warm holiday mood.

  1/2 cup shortening
  1/4 cup molasses
   1 egg
1-1/2 cups all-purpose flour
   1 cup sugar
  3/4 cup quick-cooking oats
   1 teaspoon baking soda
   1 teaspoon ground ginger
  1/4 teaspoon ground cloves
  1/4 teaspoon salt
Additional sugar

In a mixing bowl, cream shortening, molasses and egg. Combine dry ingredients; stir into creamed mixture. Roll into 1-in. balls; roll in sugar. Place on greased baking sheets. Flatten slightly with a flat-bottomed glass. Bake at 350° for 10 minutes (do not overbake). **Yield:** about 3-1/2 dozen.

CANDY CANE COOKIES
Tammy Schenk, Harlowton, Montana

These festive cookies have a rich almond flavor and a pretty sprinkling of peppermint. Their candy cane shape makes them especially appealing—it wouldn't be Christmas at my house without them!

   1 cup butter (no substitutes), softened
   1 cup confectioners' sugar
   1 egg
1-1/2 teaspoons almond extract

2-1/2 cups all-purpose flour
   1 teaspoon salt
Red food coloring
  1/2 cup crushed peppermint candy canes
  1/2 cup sugar

In a mixing bowl, cream butter and sugar. Add egg and extract; mix well. Add flour and salt; mix well. Divide dough in half; add 6-7 drops of food coloring to one half. Shape tablespoonfuls of each color of dough into 4-in. ropes. Place ropes side by side; lightly press ends together and twist. Place on ungreased baking sheets; curve top of cane down. Bake at 375° for 9-12 minutes or until lightly browned. Combine crushed candy canes and sugar; immediately sprinkle over cookies. Cool for 2 minutes; remove to wire racks to cool completely. **Yield:** 3 dozen.

CHOCOLATE HAZELNUT THUMBPRINTS
Ethel Garrison, Tacoma, Washington

Since we live in hazelnut country, I love making these special cookies for festive occasions. I usually bake two or three batches for parties and homemade gifts. They're yummy tasting and cute as can be!

  2/3 cup butter *or* margarine, softened
  1/2 cup sugar
   1 egg plus 1 egg yolk
  1/2 teaspoon vanilla extract
1-1/2 cups all-purpose flour
  1/4 cup baking cocoa
  1/2 teaspoon salt
  2/3 cup ground hazelnuts *or* filberts
  1/2 cup raspberry preserves
Confectioners' sugar

In a mixing bowl, cream butter and sugar. Add egg, yolk and vanilla; mix well. Combine flour, cocoa and salt; add a third at a time to creamed mixture, beating well after each addition. Stir in nuts. Roll into 1-in. balls; place on ungreased baking sheets. With thumb, make indentation in center of cookies; fill with 1/4 teaspoon of preserves. Bake at 350° for 10-12 minutes. Cool on wire racks. Just before serving, lightly dust with confectioners' sugar. **Yield:** about 6 dozen.

PEANUT BUTTER FINGERS
Margie Lowry, McCammon, Idaho

Always a hit with the teenagers in our house, these rich bars are sure to please the peanut butter lovers in your family. They're great for serving at holiday time.

  3/4 cup butter *or* margarine, softened
  3/4 cup sugar
  3/4 cup packed brown sugar
  3/4 cup creamy peanut butter
   2 eggs
1-1/2 teaspoons vanilla extract
1-1/2 cups all-purpose flour
1-1/2 cups quick-cooking oats
  3/4 teaspoon baking soda

1/2 teaspoon salt
1 cup (6 ounces) semisweet chocolate chips
GLAZE:
3/4 cup creamy peanut butter
1 cup confectioners' sugar
4 to 6 tablespoons milk
1 cup chopped peanuts

In a mixing bowl, cream butter and sugars. Beat in peanut butter. Add eggs, one at a time, beating well after each addition. Add vanilla. Combine flour, oats, baking soda and salt; add to creamed mixture and mix well. Pour into a greased 15-in. x 10-in. x 1-in. baking pan. Bake at 325° for 18-20 minutes or until a wooden pick inserted near the center comes out clean. Immediately sprinkle with chocolate chips and return to the oven for 2 minutes or until chips begin to soften. Spread evenly over the top. For glaze, beat peanut butter and sugar. Add enough milk to reach a spreading consistency. Spread over warm bars; sprinkle with peanuts. **Yield:** 4-5 dozen.

HOLIDAY SPRITZ COOKIES
Country Woman Test Kitchen

These crisp buttery cookies make a welcome gift or sweet party treat. Color the dough in Christmasy hues and use a cookie press to make all kinds of fun shapes.

1/2 cup butter (no substitutes), softened
1 cup sugar
1 egg
2 tablespoons milk
1/2 teaspoon vanilla extract
2-1/4 cups cake flour
1/2 teaspoon salt
1 tablespoon nonpareils
Food coloring, optional

In a mixing bowl, cream butter and sugar until fluffy. Add egg; mix well. Beat in milk and vanilla. Combine flour and salt; gradually add to creamed mixture just until combined. Stir in nonpareils and food coloring if desired. Cover and chill at least 2 hours. Fill cookie press and form into desired shapes on ungreased baking sheets. Bake at 400° for 8 minutes or until edges just begin to brown. Cool on wire racks. **Yield:** about 5 dozen.

CHEWY CINNAMON BARS
Donna Halbert, Potosi, Missouri

The cinnamon flavor's BIG in these bars. I bake them during the holidays to give as gifts to my daughters' teachers.

1/2 cup butter *or* margarine, softened
1 cup sugar
1 egg
1/2 cup all-purpose flour
1-1/4 teaspoons ground cinnamon
1/4 teaspoon salt
1 cup finely chopped pecans
Confectioners' sugar

In a mixing bowl, cream butter and sugar. Add egg; beat until light and fluffy. Combine flour, cinnamon and salt;

add to creamed mixture and beat until smooth. Stir in pecans. Spread into a greased 8-in. square baking pan. Bake at 350° for 35-40 minutes or until a wooden pick comes out clean. Cut into small bars while warm; roll in sugar. **Yield:** 3 dozen.

CHOCOLATE SNOWBALLS
Mary Lou Welsh, Hinsdale, Illinois

These dainty cookies just melt in your mouth. I enjoy making them for get-togethers when there are lots of people around to enjoy them.

3/4 cup butter *or* margarine, softened
3/4 cup packed brown sugar
1 egg
1/4 cup milk
1 teaspoon vanilla extract
2 cups all-purpose flour
1/2 cup baking cocoa
1 teaspoon baking powder
1/2 teaspoon salt
1/4 teaspoon baking soda
Confectioners' sugar

In a mixing bowl, cream butter and brown sugar. Add egg, milk and vanilla; mix well. Combine flour, cocoa, baking powder, salt and baking soda; gradually add to creamed mixture. Cover and refrigerate overnight. Shape into 1-in. balls; place 2 in. apart on ungreased baking sheets. Bake at 350° for 7-8 minutes or until tops are crackled. Remove from baking sheets; immediately roll in confectioners' sugar. Cool completely. Roll again in confectioners' sugar. **Yield:** 6 dozen.

SHORTBREAD CUTOUTS
Carole Vogel, Allison Park, Pennsylvania

Almonds give these cookies a special flavor. Use your favorite cookie cutters to make different shapes, then let the kids have a hand in adding the finishing touches.

1 cup all-purpose flour
1/2 cup blanched almonds
1/4 cup sugar
1/4 teaspoon salt
1/2 cup cold butter (no substitutes)
1 egg yolk
2 teaspoons cold water
1/4 teaspoon almond extract

In a food processor, combine flour, almonds, sugar and salt; process until almonds are finely ground. Cut butter into cubes; add to processor. Pulse on and off until mixture resembles coarse crumbs. Combine yolk, water and almond extract. With the processor running, gradually add yolk mixture; process until dough forms a ball. Wrap in plastic wrap and chill at least 30 minutes. On a lightly floured surface, roll out half of the dough to 1/4-in. thickness. Cut into desired shapes; place on ungreased baking sheets. Repeat with remaining dough. Bake at 325° for 12-14 minutes or until edges are lightly browned. Cool 1 minute before removing to wire racks; cool completely. **Yield:** 3 dozen.

SWEET TREATS! Clockwise from lower left: Sugarless Licorice Stars (p. 34), Sesame Toffee (p. 33), Deluxe Caramel Corn (p. 33), Microwave Mint Fudge (p. 33), Pulled Taffy Candy Canes (p. 33).

Seasonal Sweets

Satisfy the sweet tooth in your family with these Christmas confections—but save a few for yourself!

SESAME TOFFEE

Idalene Adams, Brainerd, Minnesota
(Pictured on page 32)

This recipe originally came from a friend in Canada. The sesame seeds add a crispy texture and unique flavor to the toffee. It makes a great gift that friends and family are always happy to receive!

> 3/4 cup sesame seeds, toasted, *divided*
>   1 cup butter (no substitutes)
>   1 cup sugar
> 1/2 cup packed brown sugar
>   3 tablespoons water
> 3/4 teaspoon baking soda

Evenly spread half of the sesame seeds in a well-greased 13-in. x 9-in. x 2-in. baking pan; set aside. In a heavy 2-1/2-qt. saucepan, melt butter. Add sugars and water; bring to a boil over medium heat, stirring constantly. Cook and stir until candy thermometer reads 290° (soft-crack stage). Remove from the heat and stir in baking soda. Pour over sesame seeds in pan. Sprinkle with remaining sesame seeds; gently press with a spatula. Cool. Break into pieces. Store in an airtight container. **Yield:** about 1-1/4 pounds.

PULLED TAFFY CANDY CANES

Sheryl O'Danne, Port Townsend, Washington
(Pictured on page 32)

My grandmother always made these at Christmastime and said her mother did, too. The soft and chewy canes have a great minty flavor. They're especially nice because the whole family can pitch in to prepare them.

> 2 cups sugar
> 1/2 cup light corn syrup
> 1/2 cup water
> 1/4 teaspoon cream of tartar
> 3/4 teaspoon peppermint extract
>   1 teaspoon red food coloring

In a large heavy saucepan over low heat, cook sugar, corn syrup, water and cream of tartar until sugar dissolves, stirring frequently. Increase heat to medium and cook until candy thermometer reads 265° (hard-ball stage), stirring occasionally. Remove from the heat; add extract. Pour half into a buttered 15-in. x 10-in. x 1-in. pan. Add food coloring to remaining mixture; mix well. Pour into another buttered 15-in. x 10-in. x 1-in. pan. Cool 5 minutes or until cool enough to handle. Butter fingers; quickly pull half of the white or red at a time until firm but pliable (the white portion will have a milky color). When taffy is ready for cutting, pull into a 1/4-in. rope. Cut into 6-in. pieces. Twist red and white pieces together; form into canes. Place on waxed paper-lined baking sheets. Cool. **Yield:** 1 to 1-1/2 dozen.

DELUXE CARAMEL CORN

Lisa Claas, Watertown, Wisconsin
(Pictured on page 32)

A batch of this colorful crunchy snack mix is perfect for gift-giving or serving at a holiday party.

> 4 quarts plain popped popcorn
> 5 cups mini pretzel twists
> 2 cups packed brown sugar
> 1 cup butter *or* margarine
> 1/2 cup dark corn syrup
> 1/2 teaspoon salt
> 1/2 teaspoon baking soda
>   1 cup salted peanuts
>   2 cups non-chocolate candy (gumdrops, Skittles, etc.)

Place popcorn and pretzels in a large bowl; set aside. In a large heavy saucepan, combine sugar, butter, corn syrup and salt; cook over medium heat, stirring occasionally, until mixture comes to a rolling boil. Cook and stir until candy thermometer reads 238° (soft-ball stage). Remove from the heat; stir in baking soda. Quickly pour over popcorn and mix thoroughly; stir in peanuts. Turn into two greased 13-in. x 9-in. x 2-in. baking pans. Bake at 200° for 20 minutes; stir. Bake 25 minutes more. Remove from the oven; add candy and mix well. Remove from pans and place on waxed paper to cool. Break into clusters. Store in airtight containers or plastic bags. **Yield:** 6-1/2 quarts.

MICROWAVE MINT FUDGE

Helen Brust, Union Mills, Indiana
(Pictured on page 32)

My family loves chocolate and mint, so I combined those favorite flavors in this quick fudge recipe.

> 1-1/2 cups sugar
>   1 can (5 ounces) evaporated milk
> 1/4 cup butter (no substitutes)
>   5 cups miniature marshmallows
>   1 package (10 ounces) mint chocolate chips
>   1 packet (1 ounce) pre-melted baking chocolate
> 1/2 cup chopped walnuts
>   1 teaspoon vanilla extract
> 1/2 teaspoon peppermint extract

In a 2-qt. microwave-safe bowl, combine sugar, milk and butter. Microwave on high until mixture comes to a full rolling boil, stirring after 2-1/2 minutes. Cook 5 minutes more, stirring after 3 minutes. Add marshmallows; stir until melted. Stir in chips and chocolate until smooth. Stir in nuts and extracts. Immediately pour into a greased 11-in. x 7-in. x 2-in. pan. Chill until firm. Cut into squares. Store in the refrigerator. **Yield:** 2-1/4 pounds. **Editor's Note:** This recipe was tested using a 700-watt microwave.

SUGARLESS LICORICE STARS

Margaret Richardson, Spring Grove, Illinois
(Pictured on page 32)

You can enjoy this candy even if you are on a restricted diet since it's sugar-free. Use small seasonal cutters to make shapes everyone will be sweet on.

    2 envelopes unflavored gelatin
    4 cups diet cherry soda, *divided*
    3 packages (.3 ounce *each*) sugar-free cherry
        gelatin
    2 teaspoons anise flavoring

In a large bowl, soften gelatin in 1/2 cup soda. In a small saucepan, bring remaining soda to a boil. Remove from the heat; add to gelatin mixture and mix well. Stir in flavored gelatin until dissolved. Add anise; mix well. If necessary, skim foam. Pour into a 13-in. x 9-in. x 2-in. pan. Chill until firm. Use small star-shaped or other holiday cutters or cut into 1-in. squares. Store in the refrigerator. **Yield:** 7-9 dozen.

FRUITY POPCORN BALLS

Helen Myron, Owosso, Michigan

In our family, these are a favorite holiday treat. I don't know who likes them better—my grown children or their children! I've included this recipe in our family cookbook.

    6 quarts plain popped popcorn
    3 cups (about 36) large marshmallows
    3 tablespoons butter *or* margarine
    3 tablespoons fruit-flavored gelatin (any flavor)

Place popcorn in a large bowl. In a medium saucepan over low heat, cook and stir marshmallows, butter and gelatin until smooth. Pour over popcorn; mix well. Butter hands and form into 3-in. balls. **Yield:** about 2 dozen.

CHOCOLATE PEANUT BUTTER CUPS

Joanne Banko, Eastlake, Ohio

I developed this recipe by combining some dessert recipes in my collection. The smooth peanut butter flavor earns rave reviews.

    2 cups (12 ounces) semisweet chocolate chips
    2 tablespoons shortening
    36 foil bonbon-size baking cups
    1 cup peanut butter
    1/2 cup nonfat dry milk powder
    1/2 cup light corn syrup
    1 teaspoon vanilla extract

In a double boiler over simmering water, or in a microwave-safe bowl, melt chocolate chips and shortening; mix well. Place a scant teaspoonful inside each foil cup and rotate it gently in the palm of your hand to coat the sides and bottom. (Use a spoon to help coat the sides if necessary.) Place cups in miniature muffin pans; chill until firm. Set remaining chocolate aside. In a medium bowl or food processor, combine peanut butter, milk powder, corn syrup and vanilla. Stir with a wooden spoon or

process until well blended. Shape into 1-in. balls; press one ball into each chocolate cup. Top with remaining melted chocolate. Chill until set. Store in the refrigerator. **Yield:** 3 dozen.

APRICOT BALLS

Marion Corliss, Littleton, New Hampshire

While they're full of good-for-you ingredients, these candies will satisfy any sweet tooth as well. I "gift-wrap" them in colorful mini muffin papers nestled in a tin.

    1-1/4 cups dried apricots
    1/3 cup nonfat dry milk powder
    1 cup flaked coconut
    1/4 cup maple syrup
    1/4 cup milk
    2 tablespoons butter *or* margarine, melted
    3/4 cup wheat germ, toasted

In a food processor, combine apricots and milk powder; pulse until apricots are finely chopped. Transfer to a medium bowl. Add coconut, syrup, milk and butter; mix well. Shape into 1-1/4-in. balls; roll in wheat germ. Cover and chill at least 2 hours. Store in the refrigerator. **Yield:** about 2 dozen.

CHOCOLATE CRUNCH PATTIES

Nancy Currie, Schaller, Iowa

This candy's so fast and easy to make that I turn out hundreds of pieces each Christmas. People are always surprised to learn that one of the ingredients is potato chips!

    2 cups (12 ounces) butterscotch chips
    1 cup (6 ounces) milk chocolate chips
    1-1/2 cups dry roasted peanuts
    1 cup crushed thick ripple-cut potato chips

In a medium microwave-safe bowl, combine butterscotch and chocolate chips. Microwave at 50% power for 2-4 minutes or until softened, stirring after each minute. Stir until smooth. Add peanuts and potato chips; mix well. Drop by teaspoonfuls onto waxed paper-lined baking sheets. Allow to harden. **Yield:** about 4 dozen. **Editor's Note:** This recipe was tested using a 700-watt microwave.

PECAN FUDGE

Linda Cousins, Oklahoma City, Oklahoma

My mother gave me this creamy fudge recipe—it's the best! I enjoy making several batches every Christmas.

    3 cups sugar
    3/4 cup butter *or* margarine
    1 can (5 ounces) evaporated milk
    2 cups (12 ounces) semisweet chocolate chips
    30 caramels, quartered
    1 jar (7 ounces) marshmallow creme
    1 cup pecan halves
    1 teaspoon vanilla extract

In a large heavy saucepan, combine the first three ingredients. Cook and stir over low heat until sugar is dissolved; bring to a full rolling boil. Boil, stirring constantly, until candy thermometer reads 234°, about 5-7 minutes. Remove from the heat; stir in chocolate chips and caramels until melted. Add remaining ingredients; stir until well blended. Pour into a greased 13-in. x 9-in. x 2-in. pan. Chill until firm. Cut into squares. **Yield:** about 4 pounds.

ICE CREAM SUNDAE CARAMELS
Arlinda Petersen, Swanton, Nebraska

These soft caramels are a hit at holiday time. I came up with the recipe using ingredients I commonly have on hand. It's a favorite!

> 2 cups sugar
> 2 cups (16 ounces) dark corn syrup
> 2 cups (1 pint) vanilla ice cream, melted, *divided*
> 1 cup butter *or* margarine
> 8 ounces chocolate confectionery coating
> 1/2 cup peanuts, finely chopped

In a heavy 4-qt. saucepan, combine sugar, corn syrup, 1 cup ice cream and butter. Cook and stir over low heat until mixture boils. Increase heat to medium; cook and stir until candy thermometer reads 242° (nearly firm-ball stage). Remove from the heat; gradually stir in remaining ice cream. Return to the heat; cook without stirring to 244° (firm-ball stage). Immediately pour, without stirring, into a buttered 13-in. x 9-in. x 2-in. baking pan. Let cool until firm. Invert candy onto a baking sheet. Melt confectionery coating in a microwave-safe bowl or in a double boiler over simmering water. Spread over candy; sprinkle with nuts. Score top into 1-in. squares. Allow chocolate to harden. Cut into 1-in. squares, following score marks. Wrap individually in waxed paper or plastic wrap. **Yield:** about 3-1/2 pounds.

CHOCOLATE-COVERED CHIPS
Marcille Meyer, Battle Creek, Nebraska

Whenever I give these candies as gifts or serve them to guests, they're conversation starters! The savory-sweet combination makes a tempting treat.

> 1 package (24 ounces) white chocolate confectionery coating
> 1 bag (14 ounces) thick ripple-cut potato chips
> 1 package (24 ounces) milk *or* dark chocolate confectionery coating

In a double boiler over simmering water, or in a microwave-safe bowl, melt white coating. Dip chips halfway in coating; shake off excess. Place on waxed paper-lined baking sheets to harden. When hardened, melt milk or dark chocolate coating and dip other half of chips. Allow to harden. **Yield:** about 4 pounds.

> • Tip: Chocolate confectionery coating is found in baking or candy sections of most grocery stores. It is sometimes labeled "almond bark" or "candy coating" and is often sold in bulk packages (1 to 1-1/2 pounds). Confectionery coating is available in white, milk and dark chocolate varieties.

CHEWY APPLE CANDIES
Roberta Dillinger, Topeka, Kansas

This chewy fruity candy is a refreshing change of pace from traditional chocolates and fudge. It keeps well in the refrigerator—if you have any left over!

> 1-1/4 cups raspberry- *or* cinnamon-flavored applesauce, *divided*
> 2 envelopes unflavored gelatin
> 2 cups sugar
> 2 teaspoons vanilla extract
> 1 cup coarsely chopped walnuts
> 1/2 cup confectioners' sugar

In a bowl, combine 1/2 cup applesauce and gelatin; set aside to soften. In a 2-qt. saucepan, bring sugar and remaining applesauce to a boil. Add gelatin mixture; return to boiling. Boil for 15 minutes, stirring constantly. Remove from the heat; stir in vanilla and nuts. Pour into a buttered 8-in. square pan. Cover and chill overnight. Cut into 1-1/2-in. x 1/2-in. pieces; roll in confectioners' sugar. Chill several hours. Store in an airtight container in the refrigerator. **Yield:** about 7 dozen.

CREATE-A-BARK
Sharon Skildem, Maple Grove, Minnesota

With a little imagination and varied ingredients, you can create a custom candy with this recipe that you'll love.

> 1 package (24 ounces) white chocolate confectionery coating
> 2 cups of one or more of the following: dessert mints, jelly beans, M&M's, sugar-coated cereal, miniature sandwich cookies, etc.

Melt the coating in a double boiler over simmering water or in a microwave-safe bowl. Stir in candy, cereal and/or cookies. Spread on a foil-lined baking sheet. Cool. Break into pieces. **Yield:** about 2 pounds.

CHOCOLATE CREAM BONBONS
Joan Lewis, Reno, Nevada

My grandmother gave me this tasty recipe when I was a girl. Some of my fondest childhood memories are of her huge kitchen and all the delicious treats she made.

> 4 cups (1 pound) confectioners' sugar
> 1 cup ground pecans *or* walnuts
> 1/2 cup plus 2 tablespoons sweetened condensed milk
> 1/4 cup butter *or* margarine, softened
> 3 cups semisweet chocolate chips
> 2 tablespoons shortening

In a mixing bowl, combine the first four ingredients; mix well. Form into 1-in. balls. Place on baking sheets. Cover and refrigerate overnight. Melt the chocolate chips and shortening in a microwave-safe bowl or in a double boiler over simmering water. Dip balls and place on waxed paper to harden. (If balls are too soft to dip, place in the freezer for a few minutes first.) **Yield:** about 6 dozen.

DAZZLING DESSERTS! Starting clockwise from top right:
Eggnog Cake Roll (p. 37), Paradise Pumpkin Pie (p. 37),
Baked Fudge Pudding (p. 37) and Walnut Wedges (p. 38).

Festive Desserts

These fun and fancy desserts are an ideal way to top off your special holiday meals.

BAKED FUDGE PUDDING
Sue Ann Chapman, Tulsa, Oklahoma
(Pictured on page 36)

This easy-to-make pudding is a true chocolate lover's delight. I always look forward to that first dishful warm from the oven. You can top it with whipped cream, spoon it over ice cream or enjoy the fudgy flavor all by itself!

 2 cups sugar
 1/2 cup all-purpose flour
 1/2 cup baking cocoa
 4 eggs
 2 teaspoons vanilla extract
 1 cup butter *or* margarine, melted
 1 cup chopped pecans
Mint chocolate chip ice cream, whipped cream,
 chopped pecans *and/or* chocolate sauce, optional

In a mixing bowl, combine sugar, flour and cocoa. Add eggs and mix well. Beat in vanilla and butter; stir in pecans. Pour into a greased 8-in. square baking pan. Place in a larger pan filled with 1 in. of hot water. Bake at 300° for 65 minutes or until set. Serve warm or at room temperature; top with ice cream, whipped cream, pecans and/or chocolate sauce if desired. **Yield:** 9 servings.

EGGNOG CAKE ROLL
Lee Herzog, Salt Lake City, Utah
(Pictured on page 36)

This festive dessert is on the menu for lots of special occasions at our house—especially Christmas. The eggnog flavor really comes through, making it a natural for holiday entertaining.

 4 eggs, *separated*
 3/4 cup sugar, *divided*
1-1/2 teaspoons vanilla extract, *divided*
 3/4 cup sifted cake flour
 3/4 teaspoon baking powder
 1/4 teaspoon salt
 1/4 teaspoon ground nutmeg
 4 tablespoons confectioners' sugar, *divided*
 4 teaspoons cornstarch
1-1/2 cups eggnog
 1 can (8 ounces) crushed pineapple, well drained
 2/3 cup quartered maraschino cherries
 1/4 cup flaked coconut
 1 cup whipping cream
Green food coloring
Additional maraschino cherries, optional

In a large mixing bowl, beat egg yolks until thick and lemon-colored, about 3 minutes. Add 1/2 cup of sugar; beat 2 minutes. Add 1 teaspoon vanilla; mix well. In another mixing bowl, beat egg whites until foamy; gradually add remaining sugar, beating until soft peaks form.

Fold into yolk mixture. Combine cake flour, baking powder, salt and nutmeg. Fold into egg mixture until no flour streaks remain. Spread batter evenly in a greased and floured 15-in. x 10-in. x 1-in. baking pan. Bake at 375° for 13-15 minutes or until cake tests done. Turn out onto a linen towel dusted with 2 tablespoons confectioners' sugar. Roll cake up in towel, starting with a short end. Cool on wire rack. Meanwhile, for filling, combine cornstarch and a small amount of eggnog in a saucepan; mix until smooth. Stir in remaining eggnog; bring to a boil, stirring constantly. Cook and stir 2 minutes more. Remove from heat; stir in remaining vanilla. Cool. Unroll cake; spread with filling. Sprinkle with pineapple, cherries and coconut; roll up again. Whip cream with remaining confectioners' sugar; tint green. Spread over outside of cake roll. Chill 3-4 hours. Garnish with cherries if desired. **Yield:** 10-12 servings.

PARADISE PUMPKIN PIE
Karen Owen, Rising Sun, Indiana
(Pictured on page 36)

Whenever I take this pie to a holiday party, potluck supper or bake sale, I take along copies of the recipe, too—I'm sure to be asked for it. With the pie's very rich taste, even a sliver is satisfying!

 1 package (8 ounces) cream cheese, softened
 1/4 cup sugar
 1/2 teaspoon vanilla extract
 1 egg
 1 unbaked pastry shell (9 inches)
FILLING:
 1 can (16 ounces) solid-pack pumpkin
 1 cup evaporated milk
 2 eggs, beaten
 1/4 cup sugar
 1/4 cup packed brown sugar
 1 teaspoon ground cinnamon
 1/4 teaspoon salt
 1/4 teaspoon ground nutmeg
TOPPING:
 2 tablespoons all-purpose flour
 2 tablespoons brown sugar
 1 tablespoon butter *or* margarine, softened
 1/2 cup chopped pecans

In a mixing bowl, beat cream cheese until smooth. Add sugar and vanilla; mix well. Add egg; beat until smooth. Spread over bottom of pie shell. Chill 30 minutes. In a mixing bowl, beat filling ingredients until smooth. Carefully pour over the cream cheese layer. Cover edge of pie with foil. Bake at 350° for 30 minutes. Remove foil; bake 25 minutes longer. Meanwhile, mix flour, brown sugar and butter until crumbly; stir in pecans. Sprinkle over pie. Bake 10-15 minutes more or until a knife inserted near the center comes out clean. Cool on a wire rack. Store in the refrigerator. **Yield:** 6-8 servings.

WALNUT WEDGES
Connie Meinke, Neenah, Wisconsin
(Pictured on page 36)

When you want to serve something light but fancier than cookies, these dainty treats make a beautiful dessert. With a prepared pie crust, they're easy…yet have a special holiday look—the perfect combination for a busy time of year.

Pastry for double-crust pie
    1 cup finely chopped walnuts
  1/3 cup sugar
    2 tablespoons honey
    1 teaspoon ground cinnamon
    1 teaspoon lemon juice
    1 to 2 tablespoons milk
  1/2 cup semisweet chocolate chips
    1 teaspoon shortening

Roll out bottom crust to a 10-1/2-in. circle; place on an ungreased baking sheet. Combine nuts, sugar, honey, cinnamon and lemon juice; spread over crust. Roll out remaining pastry and place over nuts. With fork tines, seal edges together and pierce holes in top. Brush with milk. Bake at 375° for 15-20 minutes or until lightly browned. Cool for 10 minutes. Cut into 16-20 wedges. Cool completely. In a small saucepan, melt chocolate chips and shortening over low heat; drizzle over wedges. **Yield: 16-20 servings.**

CHOCOLATE CREPES WITH CRANBERRY SAUCE
Lynda Sarkisian, Inman, South Carolina

With its unique flavor and festive look, this dessert has become a "must" for Christmas at our house. It's an elegant addition to the dinner table.

    1 package (3.4 ounces) instant vanilla pudding mix
2-1/2 cups milk, *divided*
    1 carton (8 ounces) frozen whipped topping, thawed
    2 tablespoons vegetable oil
    3 eggs
1-1/2 teaspoons vanilla extract
  1/4 cup sugar
1-1/2 cups all-purpose flour
    2 tablespoons baking cocoa
  1/8 teaspoon salt
CRANBERRY SAUCE:
1-1/2 cups fresh *or* frozen cranberries
    1 cup cranberry juice
  1/2 cup packed brown sugar
1-1/2 teaspoons cornstarch
  1/2 teaspoon grated orange peel
  1/4 teaspoon ground nutmeg
  1/8 teaspoon salt
    2 tablespoons butter *or* margarine
    1 teaspoon vanilla extract

In a bowl, whisk the pudding mix and 1 cup of milk until smooth. Fold in whipped topping; cover and chill. In a blender container, combine oil, eggs, vanilla, sugar, flour, cocoa, salt and remaining milk; process until smooth. Let stand for 20 minutes. Meanwhile, combine the first seven sauce ingredients in a small saucepan; bring to a boil. Reduce heat and simmer until smooth and thickened, stirring constantly, about 15 minutes. Remove from the heat; stir in the butter and vanilla. Keep warm. Heat a lightly greased 6-in. skillet over medium heat until hot. Pour 3 tablespoons crepe batter into skillet and swirl quickly so bottom is evenly covered. Cook until top appears dry and bottom is lightly browned; turn and cook 15-20 seconds longer. Remove and keep warm. Repeat with remaining batter. To serve, fold crepes in quarters; place three on a dessert plate. Top with chilled pudding mixture and warm sauce. **Yield: 6-8 servings.**

ICE CREAM BALLS
Ann Marie Woodhull, Cedar Springs, Michigan

This is a fun and easy dessert to fix for Christmas gatherings—even the kids can help. The cereal adds a crunchy texture to the ice cream and makes an everyday treat something special.

1-1/2 cups Corn Chex cereal, crushed
  1/4 cup packed brown sugar
    2 tablespoons butter *or* margarine, melted
  1/4 cup finely chopped walnuts
    1 pint vanilla ice cream, softened
Hot fudge *or* caramel ice cream topping, optional

In a shallow bowl, combine cereal, sugar and butter; mix well. Add nuts. Shape ice cream into 1-in. balls; roll in cereal mixture until well coated. Freeze for at least 1 hour. If desired, serve with fudge or caramel ice cream topping. **Yield: 12-16 balls.**

ALMOND CREAM PARFAITS
Lynn McAllister, Mt. Ulla, North Carolina

Cooking is one of my favorite hobbies—particularly during the Christmas season. These parfaits are a great way to top off holiday meals. They have a sweet almond flavor but aren't too heavy and filling.

    1 cup sugar, *divided*
  1/4 cup cornstarch
    3 cups milk
    4 egg yolks
    1 tablespoon butter *or* margarine
  1/2 teaspoon almond extract
  3/4 cup chopped toasted almonds
  1/2 cup shortbread cookie crumbs
    1 cup whipping cream
    6 to 8 maraschino cherries

In a medium saucepan, combine 3/4 cup sugar and cornstarch. Gradually add milk; cook and stir over medium heat until thickened and bubbly. In a small bowl, beat egg yolks; gradually add 1 cup of hot milk mixture. Return all to pan. Bring to a boil; boil for 1-2 minutes or until thickened. Add butter and extract; mix well. Chill for 1 hour or until cool. Add almonds. Pour into six to eight parfait glasses; sprinkle with cookie crumbs. In a mixing bowl, beat cream and remaining sugar until soft peaks form. Spoon over parfaits. Chill. Just before serving, garnish with cherries. **Yield: 6-8 servings.**

Gifts from the Kitchen

Wrap up one of these tempting foods and give a gift that's sure to be in good taste.

HERB BUTTER
Dixie Terry, Marion, Illinois

This savory butter makes a thoughtful and versatile gift at holiday time. It's great spread on French bread or chicken before baking, or tossed with hot cooked vegetables or pasta.

>   2 cups butter *or* margarine, softened
> 1/4 cup minced fresh parsley
>   2 tablespoons minced garlic cloves
>   4 teaspoons Italian seasoning
>   1 teaspoon crushed red pepper flakes

In a mixing bowl, combine all ingredients. Beat until well blended. Cover and store in the refrigerator. **Yield:** 2 cups.

SAUCE CHRISTINE
Harvey Robert, Stuart, Florida

This recipe is named after my great-grandmother, who originally developed it. The spicy fruit flavor goes well with pork roast or ham or drizzled over ice cream.

>   1 can (16-1/2 ounces) pitted dark sweet bing
>   cherries, undrained
> 1-1/2 cups applesauce
>   1/2 cup sugar
>   1/2 teaspoon ground cinnamon

In a 1-qt. saucepan, combine all ingredients; bring to a boil, stirring constantly. Reduce heat; simmer, uncovered, for 1 hour. **Yield:** 2-1/4 cups.

TURTLE ICE CREAM SAUCE
Marci Cullen, Milton, Wisconsin

Making this rich caramel-fudge sauce is a family affair at our house—the kids love to unwrap the caramels! The sauce can be made ahead and frozen.

>   2 cups butter *or* margarine
>   2 cans (12 ounces *each*) evaporated milk
>   2 cups sugar
> 1/3 cup dark corn syrup
> 1/8 teaspoon salt
>   2 cups (12 ounces) semisweet chocolate chips
>   1 bag (14 ounces) caramels
>   1 teaspoon vanilla extract

In a large saucepan or Dutch oven, combine the first seven ingredients in order given. Cook, stirring constantly, over medium-low heat until the caramels are melted and mixture is smooth (do not boil). Reduce heat to low. With an electric hand mixer on medium speed, beat in vanilla; continue beating for 5 minutes. Beat on high for 2 minutes. Remove from the heat and cool for 30 minutes (sauce will thicken as it cools). Pour into glass or plastic food storage containers. Store in the refrigerator. Serve warm or cold. **Yield:** 9 cups.

WILD RICE PILAF MIX
Margaret Snider, Guernsey, Saskatchewan

We exchange homemade gifts in our family—I give this tasty mix to relatives and friends. It goes well with a variety of entrees and it's a handy side dish to serve when guests drop in.

>   3 cups uncooked wild rice
>   2 cups dried lentils
>   2 cups raisins
>   1 cup medium barley
> 1/2 cup sunflower seeds
> 1/4 cup beef bouillon granules
>   3 tablespoons dried parsley flakes
>   3 tablespoons dried minced onion
>   2 tablespoons dried minced garlic
>   1 tablespoon dried basil
>   1 tablespoon salt
> 1/2 teaspoon ground cinnamon
> 1/2 teaspoon pepper

In a large bowl, combine all ingredients; mix well. Store in an airtight container. To make two servings, combine 1/3 cup mix and 1 cup water in a small saucepan; bring to a boil. Reduce heat; cover and simmer for 50 minutes or until rice and barley are tender. **Yield:** 9 cups mix.

MICROWAVE PEACH BUTTER
Linda Haley, Holt, Michigan

I often make this quick and easy recipe—it can even be made ahead of time and frozen. For gift-giving, I decorate the jar lids with Christmas fabric, lace and ribbons.

>   4 cans (16 ounces *each*) peach halves *or* slices,
>   drained
>   1 box (1-3/4 ounces) powdered fruit pectin
> 1-1/2 teaspoons ground cinnamon
>   1/2 teaspoon ground allspice
> 4-1/2 cups sugar

Place peaches in a food processor or blender; process until smooth. In a large microwave-safe bowl, combine the peaches, pectin, cinnamon and allspice; mix well. Cover with waxed paper and microwave on high for 7-8 minutes or until mixture just starts to bubble, stirring every 2 minutes. Stir in sugar; microwave on high for 8-9 minutes or until mixture comes to a rolling boil, stirring after 6 minutes. Microwave on high for 1 minute. Pour hot into hot jars or freezer containers, leaving 1/2-in. headspace. Cool slightly. Cover with tight-fitting lids. Refrigerate or freeze. May be refrigerated for 3 weeks or frozen up to 3 months. **Yield:** 8 half-pints. **Editor's Note:** This recipe was tested in a 700-watt microwave.

CHRISTMAS GIFTS FROM THE KITCHEN.
Clockwise from top right: Spicy Mustard (p. 41), Fire-and-Ice Pickles (p. 41), Pear Raspberry Jam (p. 41), and Minty Hot Chocolate (p. 41).

Minty Hot Chocolate

SPICY MUSTARD

Pear Raspberry Jam

Pear Raspberry Jam

Pear Raspberry Jam

FIRE-AND-ICE PICKLES
Myra Innes, Auburn, Kansas
(Pictured on page 40)

These sweet and spicy pickles are great on a sandwich or all by themselves as a snack. The recipe is an easy way to dress up store-bought pickles and make them a special treat!

    2 jars (32 ounces *each*) dill pickle slices *or* spears
    4 cups sugar
    1 tablespoon hot pepper sauce
    1/2 teaspoon crushed red pepper flakes
    3 garlic cloves, peeled

Drain and discard juice from pickles. In a large bowl, combine pickles, sugar, pepper sauce and pepper flakes; mix well. Cover and let stand 2 hours, stirring occasionally. Spoon pickles and liquid into 3 pint-size jars; add a garlic clove to each. Cover and refrigerate 1 week before serving. Store in the refrigerator. **Yield:** 3 pints.

SPICY MUSTARD
Joyce Lonsdale, Unionville, Pennsylvania
(Pictured on page 40)

When I make this mustard, I add fresh horseradish from our garden and vinegar seasoned with homegrown tarragon.

    1/2 cup tarragon *or* cider vinegar
    1/2 cup water
    1/4 cup olive *or* vegetable oil
    2 tablespoons prepared horseradish
    1/2 teaspoon lemon juice
    1 cup ground mustard
    1/2 cup sugar
    1/2 teaspoon salt

In a blender or food processor, combine all ingredients. Process for 1 minute. Scrape down the sides of the container and process for 30 seconds. Transfer to a small saucepan and let stand 10 minutes. Cook over low heat, stirring constantly, until bubbly. Cool completely. If a thinner mustard is desired, stir in an additional 1-2 tablespoons water. Pour into small containers with tight-fitting lids. Store in the refrigerator. **Yield:** 1-1/2 cups.

PEAR RASPBERRY JAM
Susan Burton, Yakima, Washington
(Pictured on page 40)

I give this sweet and tangy jam as a Christmas gift. In this part of the country, pears and raspberries are in plentiful supply, but frozen berries work just as well.

    2 cups coarsely chopped peeled ripe pears (about
      2 medium)
    2 cups fresh *or* frozen raspberries
    6 cups sugar
    2 tablespoons lemon juice
    2 teaspoons finely grated orange peel
    1 pouch (3 ounces) liquid fruit pectin

In a large kettle, combine the first five ingredients; bring to a full rolling boil, stirring constantly. Quickly stir in

pectin; return to a full rolling boil. Boil for 1 minute, stirring constantly. Remove from the heat; skim off foam. Pour hot into hot jars, leaving 1/4-in. headspace. Adjust caps. Process 15 minutes in a boiling-water bath. **Yield:** 6 half-pints.

MINTY HOT CHOCOLATE
Esther Lambright, Shipshewana, Indiana
(Pictured on page 40)

This hot chocolate mix features a tasty blend of mint and malt. We enjoy some each holiday season—especially after an evening of caroling!

    2 cups chocolate-flavored malted milk powder,
      divided
    1 cup butter mints
    3 cups nonfat dry milk powder
    1-1/2 cups instant hot cocoa mix

In a blender or food processor, combine 1 cup malted milk powder and mints; process until smooth. Pour into a large bowl. Add dry milk, cocoa mix and remaining malted milk powder; mix well. Store in airtight containers. To make one serving, add 1/4 cup mix to 3/4 cup boiling water; stir until dissolved. **Yield:** 6-3/4 cups mix.

FROSTED HAZELNUTS
Kathleen Lutz, Steward, Illinois

Serve these spicy-sweet nuts at your holiday party or buffet—they're a tempting snack for any occasion.

    2 egg whites
    1 cup sugar
    2 tablespoons water
    1 teaspoon salt
    1/2 teaspoon *each* ground cloves, cinnamon and
      allspice
    4 cups hazelnuts *or* filberts

In a medium bowl, lightly beat egg whites. Add sugar, water, salt and spices; mix well. Let stand 5 minutes or until sugar is dissolved. Add hazelnuts; stir gently to coat. Spread into two greased 15-in. x 10-in. x 1-in. baking pans. Bake at 275° for 50-60 minutes or until crisp. Remove to waxed paper to cool. Store in airtight containers. **Yield:** 6 cups.

VANILLA-ALMOND COFFEE
Tina Christensen, Addison, Illinois

This recipe is perfect for any coffee lover. Instead of buying flavored coffees, I make my own using flavored extracts for baking. You can prepare this with decaffeinated coffee, too.

    1 pound ground coffee (not instant)
    1 ounce vanilla extract
    1 ounce almond extract

Place coffee in a large jar with tight-fitting lid. Add extracts. Cover and shake well. Store in the refrigerator. Prepare coffee as usual. **Yield:** 1 pound.

Cake's Abloom with Holiday Cheer

YOUR guests won't be able to resist sampling a piece of this dessert that's all decked out for the season. Whip up the White Chocolate Holiday Cake below or use your own favorite recipe. Then follow the instructions on the next page to add the pretty edible poinsettia decorations. It's sure to be a hit at your special holiday gathering.

WHITE CHOCOLATE HOLIDAY CAKE
Kim Van Rheenen, Mendota, Illinois

At our house, we always bake a birthday cake for Baby Jesus on Christmas Eve. The delicious tradition helps re-mind us all of the true meaning of the season that we are celebrating.

> 1 cup butter *or* margarine, softened
> 2 cups sugar, *divided*
> 4 eggs, room temperature, *separated*
> 1-1/2 cups buttermilk
> 1 package (6 ounces) white chocolate baking squares, melted and cooled
> 1 teaspoon vanilla extract
> 2-1/2 cups cake flour
> 1-1/2 teaspoons baking powder
> 1/2 teaspoon salt
> 1/4 teaspoon baking soda
> 1 cup chopped pecans

> 1 cup flaked coconut
> FROSTING:
> 1-1/2 cups butter (no substitutes), softened
> 6 cups confectioners' sugar
> 1 tablespoon vanilla extract
> 3 to 4 tablespoons milk
> Poinsettia clay (page 43), optional

In a mixing bowl, cream butter and 1-1/2 cups of sugar. Add egg yolks, one at a time, beating well after each addition; set aside. Gradually stir buttermilk into white chocolate; add vanilla. Combine flour, baking powder, salt and baking soda. Add dry ingredients alternately with buttermilk mixture to creamed mixture;

mix well. Beat egg whites until soft peaks form. Gradually add remaining sugar, beating until stiff peaks form; fold into batter. Fold in pecans and coconut. Pour into three greased and floured 9-in. round baking pans. Bake at 350° for 30-35 minutes or until cake tests done. Cool in pans 10 minutes before removing to wire racks; cool completely. For frosting, beat butter, sugar, vanilla and 3 tablespoons milk at low speed in a mixing bowl until moistened. Increase speed to medium and beat for 1-1/2 minutes, adding additional milk to reach a spreading consistency. Spread between layers and over the top and sides of cake. Decorate with poinsettia clay if desired. **Yield:** 12-16 servings.

EDIBLE POINSETTIA CHRISTMAS CLAY

Patterns on this page
1/3 cup light corn syrup
Red and green liquid or paste food coloring
  10 ounces white chocolate confectionery coating*, melted (about 1-3/4 cups chopped)

Divide corn syrup between two bowls. Tint one bowl with red food coloring to a deep shade, and tint the other with green. Stir half of the melted chocolate coating into each bowl, stirring just until blended. Spread each on a sheet of waxed paper to 1/3-in. thickness (about a 4-in. square). Let stand, uncovered, at room tempera-

ture for 2-3 hours or until dry to the touch. Remove clay from waxed paper and gather into a ball. Wrap tightly in plastic wrap; let stand overnight. Use immediately or store for up to 2 weeks. *For a tip on purchasing confectionery coating, see page 35.

To make cake top poinsettia: To cut out each leaf or petal, knead a portion of the appropriate color clay until pliable but not soft. Roll clay between sheets of waxed paper to 1/8-in. thickness. Trace the patterns onto another piece of waxed paper and cut out. Place patterns on rolled-out clay and use sharp knife to cut around edge of patterns.

For bottom leaves, cut out three large leaves from rolled-out green clay. Set aside remainder. With the point of a knife, score the veins in the leaves as shown on pattern but do not cut all the way through. Place the large leaves centered on top of the cake with center points touching.

For the bottom flower petals, cut out five large flower petals from rolled-out red clay. Set aside remainder. With the point of a knife, add veins as done with bottom leaves. Curve the point of each petal up and shape as shown in photo on page 42. Matching centers, place these petals over the leaves, positioning them evenly around and adding a 1/4-in. ball of red clay under the larger curves of the petals.

For the top flower petals, cut out three small flower petals from the rolled-out red clay, rolling out additional clay as needed. With the point of a knife, add veins as done with bottom leaves. Curve the point of the

petal up and shape as shown. Matching centers over centers of bottom petals, add the top petals between the bottom petals evenly around the top.

For flower stamens, form 3/8-in. balls of green clay. Place several in center of flower, covering all petal centers.

To decorate the sides of the cake (as on page 42): For side leaves, cut out 14 small leaves from rolled-out green clay. With the point of a knife, add veins as done with bottom leaves. Form leaves into seven sets of two leaves each, making centers match and sides overlap as shown in photo. Place sets evenly around the base of cake. Make a small (1/4-in.) ball of red clay and press onto the point where the leaves meet.

To decorate cake sides with additional flowers (as shown on front cover): Cut out 15 additional small flower petals from rolled-out red clay. With the point of a knife, add veins as done with bottom leaves. Curve and shape as shown in cover photo. For each side flower, form a group of three small petals, bringing centers together and overlapping edges as shown on cover. Set aside.

Cut out five small leaves from rolled-out green clay. With the point of a knife, add veins as done with bottom leaves. Add one small leaf to the group of three petals and position on the side of the cake. Repeat with remaining petals and leaves, forming five side flower groupings around the base of the cake.

Add flower stamens, forming several 1/4-in. balls to add to the center of each flower.　　　　▲

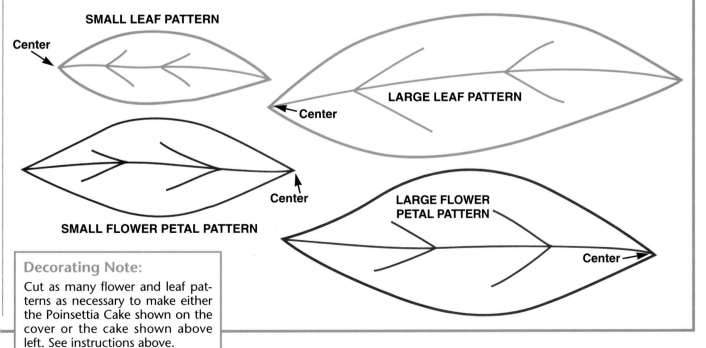

SMALL LEAF PATTERN

Center

LARGE LEAF PATTERN

Center

Center

SMALL FLOWER PETAL PATTERN

LARGE FLOWER PETAL PATTERN

Center

Decorating Note:
Cut as many flower and leaf patterns as necessary to make either the Poinsettia Cake shown on the cover or the cake shown above left. See instructions above.

These Students Learn Tasteful Yule Lesson

AT holiday time, Ellen Wages' second-grade classroom in Vancleave, Mississippi turns into a tantalizing construction zone. The taste-tempting project? Decorating gingerbread houses!

For Ellen, it's a natural way to combine two of her favorite pursuits. "I enjoy teaching, but when I went back to it 7 years ago, I found I really missed the baking I'd been able to do at home," the mother of five relates.

Now, every year in her own kitchen, Ellen lays a good foundation beforehand for her two dozen eager architects by mixing up enough dough to make two houses. "I add extra ginger to the recipe," she notes. "It really fills the classroom with the spicy fragrance of Christmas!"

Her engineer husband, Jerry, lends his talents by constructing a heavy cardboard shell with a reinforced roof to support the dough and icing for each house.

Once she's put together the cookie canvases, her students are ready to add edible embellishments—candy, ice cream cones and even cereal!—that they bring from home for their classy confectionary construction.

"The roof is the most important part," Ellen notes. "I make it the night before for the students to apply. A waffle roof's especially neat and easy."

Down at ground level, the "landscaping" doesn't lack for attention either.

"Charlotte Bosarge, my teaching assistant, and I pipe ice cream cones with green icing to serve as trees," Ellen observes sweetly. "Pretzels make wonderful fences. And Tootsie Rolls are perfect for the woodpile or Yule log."

Once the masterpieces are complete, each roof is dusted with powdered sugar. Then the decorators help clean up—by devouring some of the leftovers!

The gingerbread project has cooked up lots of sweet memories for Ellen and her students alike. "Every year brings a new story for our Christmas album," she comments. "I hope I can carry on this project for a long time."

With the scrumptious fringe benefit her willing workers enjoy, *that* should be no problem. Just before Christmas vacation begins, Ellen draws the names of two lucky pupils—who each get to take a house home for the holidays! ▲

CONSTRUCTION CREW! Ellen Wages and second-grade class proudly pose with handiwork.

ELLEN'S EDIBLE GINGERBREAD HOUSE

The Country Woman test kitchen staff adapted Ellen Wages' pretty gingerbread house (see the story on opposite page)...and came up with this petite version. Unlike Ellen's larger classroom house, it doesn't need to be constructed around a cardboard shell.

DOUGH:
    1/2 cup butter *or* margarine,
        softened
    3/4 cup packed dark brown
        sugar
    3/4 cup dark molasses
        1 egg
        2 teaspoons ground ginger
        1 teaspoon ground cloves
    1/4 teaspoon salt
    3-1/2 to 4 cups all-purpose flour

In a mixing bowl, beat butter until fluffy. Beat in sugar, molasses, egg, ginger, cloves and salt until well mixed. Gradually add flour, 1 cup at a time, until dough can be formed into a ball. Using remaining flour, lightly flour a wooden board. Turn dough onto the board; knead until smooth and not sticky, adding more flour if needed. Cover and chill several hours or overnight.

Meanwhile, referring to diagrams below, cut patterns out of a shoe box or cardboard. Line a baking sheet with foil and lightly grease foil. Lay a damp towel on the counter; place prepared pan on towel (to prevent slipping). Using a heavily floured rolling pin, roll out half of the dough directly on the baking sheet to a rectangle about 1/8 in. thick. Position the patterns at least 1/2 in. apart on dough. Cut out two of each pattern piece with a sharp knife or pizza cutter; remove pattern. Remove dough scraps; cover and save to re-roll if needed.

Bake at 350° for 15 minutes or until edges just begin to brown. Do not overbake. Remove from oven; immediately replace patterns on dough. Cut around the edges to trim off excess cookie if necessary. Cool 10 minutes or until pieces begin to firm up. Carefully remove to a wire rack to cool completely. Repeat with remaining dough and patterns. Dough scraps may be cut into gingerbread people and used to decorate house. **Yield:** 1 house.

ICING AND ASSEMBLY:
        4 cups (1 pound)
            confectioners' sugar
        3 tablespoons meringue
            powder*
        5 to 6 tablespoons warm water
Decorating bag
Large dot (#12) decorating tip
Spice jars
Green food coloring
Starlight mints (shingles)
**Caramels (chimney and mailbox
    base)**
Sugar cones (trees)
Thin butter ring cookie (wreath)
**Red-hot candies (ornaments on
    trees, bow on wreath)**
**Colored sprinkles (decorating
    wreath and trees)**
Red licorice (doorway)
**Fruit-stripe gum (shutters and
    mailbox flag)**
Sixlets (windows and walkway)
Fruit leather (walkway)
**Tootsie Rolls (large for mailbox,
    small for woodpile)**
Thin pretzel stick (mailbox post)
Mini pretzel twists (fence)

In a mixing bowl, beat the sugar, meringue powder and 4 tablespoons water on low until blended. Beat on high for 8-10 minutes or until stiff peaks form, adding additional water, 1 tablespoon at a time, if needed. Place a damp paper towel over icing bowl and cover tightly until ready to use. *Meringue powder is available where cake decorating supplies are sold. Or you may order it by contacting Wilton Enterprises, 2240 W. 75th St., Woodridge IL 60517; 1-708/963-7100.

To assemble the frame of the house: Test your cookie pieces to make sure they fit together snugly. If necessary, file carefully with a serrated knife or an emery board to make them fit. Fill decorating bag two-thirds full with icing. Beginning with the front of the house, squeeze a 3/8-in.-wide strip of icing onto the bottom edge of the front piece. Position on a cutting board or display surface, at least 3 in. from the front edge of the base. Prop it upright with spice jars for 2-3 minutes or until icing hardens; remove jars.

To add the sides and the back: Squeeze icing on the lower edge of one side piece and side edge of the front piece. Align pieces at a right angle, making sure they are as tight as possible. Repeat with the other side. Squeeze icing on the bottom and side edges of the back piece; position with the other assembled pieces. For added stability, squeeze icing along the *inside* edge of all pieces and corners.

To assemble the roof: Working with one side at a time, squeeze icing on the upper edge of the slant on one side of both the front and back pieces. Also squeeze icing on the adjoining side piece. Carefully place one roof piece on the slants so that the roof's peak is even with the points of the front and back (there will be a small overhang front and back). Repeat with other roof piece.

To decorate: Add mints to roof, attaching with icing. For the chimney, stack caramels along one side of house, using icing between; top with an icing "smoke cloud". Add green food coloring to a portion of icing; frost sugar cones and butter cookie to make trees and wreath. Decorate with red-hots and sprinkles. Referring to photo and using candies and cookies as directed in list of ingredients, add doorway, wreath, windows, shutters, walkway, trees, logs, mailbox and fence. ▲

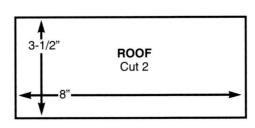

FRONT/BACK
Cut 2

5-1/2"

3-1/2"

6"

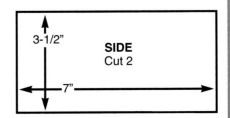

ROOF
Cut 2

3-1/2"

8"

SIDE
Cut 2

3-1/2"

7"

Country Decorating...

SIGNS OF THE SEASON appear inside and out at home of Brenda Schroeder (above left), who packs parlor with host of holiday accents. Sporty tree spruces up son Jeremy's room (right).

Christmas Colors This House...Top to Bottom!

WHEN Brenda Schroeder dresses up her house for the holidays, simply decking the halls won't do. The season's spirit overflows in almost every corner of her Shelby, Ohio home.

"I've always loved crafts and especially enjoyed decorating," smiles the farm wife and mother of three sons. "As a child, I helped my mom pick out wallpaper and curtains.

"I liked to arrange things on the walls even then," she adds. "And I was a girl who actually had fun setting the table! Now, with my own home, I enjoy all those things more than ever."

Looking around the Schroeders' 130-year-old brick homestead, it's apparent Brenda still delights in the details. The entrance is wrapped in a garland of greenery and trimmed with fes-

tive red bows. Antique wagon wheels aren't overlooked either—they wear a sprig of holiday cheer.

In the kitchen, a pretty poinsettia tablecloth and a grapevine tree draped with baby's breath, holly leaves and glittering white lights complement her country decor.

"Nothing is more fun for me than planning a menu and setting a nice table," she informs. "When people walk into your home and see an inviting table, they feel welcome right away."

Shedding a soft glow that can be enjoyed inside and out, the family's Christmas tree is nestled in front of the living room windows. The festive focus of the room, it's decorated with dozens of handmade ornaments and a beaded garland, then topped off with an angel

watching over the holiday doings.

A greenery wreath on the wall helps ring in the season. Artificial apples, white-tipped pinecones and a big red bow encircle the living room with natural beauty.

Not to be outdone, the Schroeder boys boast their own brand of holiday decorating. "They have their very own Christmas trees in their bedrooms," Brenda notes with a grin.

Matthew and Mark's bedroom features a farm theme with chickens, sheep and cows adorning their tree. A cozy quilt, some cuddly barnyard pals and mini versions of the tractors their dad, Steve, drives on the farm are at home underneath.

FESTIVE FARMSTEAD features garlands of greenery for greeting guests (above left). Christmasy cupboard in dining room groans with goodies of the season (above), while sons Matthew and Mark wait for Santa in bedroom with real rural feel (below).

Jeremy's sprightly spruce exhibits his chief interest—sports. It's ringed in a garland of red beads and popcorn. A stadium blanket and football helmet show lots of spirit as well.

Even the bathroom has a holiday outlook—thanks to colorful towels, a beautiful bowl brimming with spicy potpourri and a mini tree trimmed with tiny hand soap ornaments.

"I just love Christmas," Brenda cheerfully sums up. And, it's easy to see from a peek at her place this time of year, the type she's particularly enamored of is a home-style one! ▲

In Girl's Eyes, Grandpa Was Right Jolly Old Elf

By Fern Houston Crawford of St. George, Utah

hen I was a little girl, our family owned the oldest store in Panguitch, Utah. Like most such country establishments, it carried nearly everything imaginable…from sugar and shoelaces to fireplace matches and farm machinery.

That's not all—it also was home to Santa Claus himself!

You see, every Christmas season, my father would slip china-headed dolls and other toys in the grocery bags of customers he knew couldn't afford many luxuries for their little ones. He'd also pack up the fixings for a special dinner and send them to less fortunate local families.

More than that, though, to the children of our town, he *was* Santa—playing that role for many years in Panguitch's annual ceremony welcoming the jolly old elf.

Finally, for us Houstons as well, Santa and my father were interchangeable. Each Christmas, he also slipped into his costume for our family festivities. One merry season, all that role playing led to a memorable confirmation of the magic of Christmas.

At long last, Dad had decided to "retire". He urged the other members of the Lions Club (who had taken on the responsibility of organizing the arrival event) to find a new Claus.

His children were all grown, he told them, and the grandkids were getting old enough to start recognizing him.

But, as Christmas Eve drew closer, several club members came to the house. Would he consider taking on the role just *one* more time? Dad relented and donned the duds again.

After the town celebration welcoming Father Christmas, Dad was at home relaxing in front of the fireplace. Suddenly, he heard his granddaughter Allyson—one of those he'd been concerned about identifying him—burst through the kitchen door.

"Grandma! Grandma! Guess what?" she shouted excitedly. "It *was* the real Santa. I know—he looked just like Grandpa!"

Dad silently chuckled…and concluded that, in a way, his secret was still safe after all! ▲

Santa Lives

Jolly old St. Nicholas,
Lend your ear this way.
There are those who say you're not—
How'd they get that way?

So long as children's eyes light up,
So long as parents care,
So long as hope eternal springs…
We'll know that you are there.

So long as moon and stars look down
Across white fields of snow,
Will reindeer flash across the sky
One shiny nose aglow.

Jolly old St. Nicholas,
Lend your ear this way.
Love and hope and childlike faith
Will prove you're here to stay.
        —**Madeleine K. Robinson**
        Burlington, Wisconsin

Doll Maker's Many Santas Are Claus For Celebration

WHILE everyone likes Santa Claus, to Silvia Hendershott, he's a real doll—some 150 times every year. Since the early '80's, this holiday-loving country lady from Blue Bell, Pennsylvania has turned out over 1,800 of the fun Christmas figures!

"Many of my Santa dolls are created from family interests—the patriot, the fisherman, the engineer," she reveals. "Sometimes, an old postcard will inspire a new Santa. Mostly, though, I just wonder, 'What would Santa like to do or be?'"

Whatever the answer, her Santas don't spring to life speedily. "First," she says, "I hand-mold a face from mache clay. That part of the process alone can be spread out over 5 to 6 months.

"Meanwhile, I cut the different fabrics, make clothes, hunt antique toys at flea markets, design new patterns and wire bodies. When a face is finally ready, it can take me anywhere from a day to a week to put a doll together."

For artful assists with her jolly old elves, Silvia can always count on her helpful clan. Husband Don, noted on his own for his wooden birds, hand-carves Santa accessories—ice skates, birds, arks and more. Daughter Karen contributes her illustrator talents plus has grown

gourds for Silvia's Harvest Santa.

Playing their part, children Paul, Cheryl and Brenda visit to lend a hand at the annual events at which Silvia exhibits.

With so much family feeling behind what she does, it's not surprising that Silvia emphasizes the personal touch.

"Special orders are exciting," she smiles. "For instance, we might add bears for someone who loves them. Or maybe we'll snuggle a birthday cake in Santa's pack. Finding that special something can be as much fun as making the Santa.

"I've made wedding Santas carrying decorated trees with gifts for the home. There's even a miniature bride and groom that Don and I cast ourselves."

Silvia's festive figures are also seasoned travelers, spreading holiday cheer as far away as the Netherlands, Germany, Australia and New Zealand.

And *that* makes Silvia happy. "My Santa dolls have given me a wonderful life," she beams. "They keep that special Christmas spirit alive for me…all year-round."

Editor's Note: *For more information, send a self-addressed stamped envelope to Silvia Hendershott, 1801 Pulaski Dr., Blue Bell PA 19422.* ▲

QUICK AS ST. NICK is Silvia Hendershott (top), who handcrafts 150 smile-starting Santas a year! Her clever Clauses come in all sizes, colors, costumes.

The Year the 'Animals' Spoke, The Heart of Christmas Shone

By Juanene Rhodes of Omro, Wisconsin

DID YOU KNOW at a certain magical time of year, animals can "talk"? In the real spirit of Christmas, they did once in my family's barn…and they can at your place, too. Let me explain…

When our daughters were young, one of their favorite storybooks was *The Animals' Christmas Eve.*

The simple tale is set in a barn on the night before Christmas. At the stroke of midnight, an angel blesses the creatures with the ability to speak in human voices, and they proceed to tell the Nativity story from their point of view.

Over the years, I spent many evenings talking over the tale with our girls …who, every now and then, wondered out loud if there was any truth to it.

As I tucked them in one night after another such chat, an inspiration suddenly struck—what would the children think if the animals in *our* barn began talking on Christmas Eve? Hurrying downstairs, I shared the idea with my husband, Tony. "Operation Animal Eve" was enthusiastically born!

Christmas in July

Luckily, it was only July, so we still had plenty of time to fine-tune our plan.

I started by sending short scripts and audiotapes to friends and relatives living some distance from us. That way, the girls would be less likely to recognize anyone's voice.

Uncle Ken agreed to be the horse—his deep tone fit the part perfectly. Aunt Gaye opted for the ponies and sheep. Mitch and Joy covered the cows' and donkey's roles.

My sister took on the part of the cats, and a friend read the rabbits' lines. Another lent her voice to the chickens, while an old neighbor volunteered for the dog's part.

After everyone returned their completed tapes, I spent a little time in the barn recording animal sounds. Once that was finished, Tony took everything to the local technical school sound studio and mixed the final version together.

Looked Forward to Faces

We were both thrilled with the results. Christmas Eve couldn't come quick enough! How we looked forward to seeing the looks on our daughters' faces as their favorite story came to life.

When December 24 finally arrived, Tony made the big announcement: "This year, we're going to stay up until midnight to see if the animals really *do* tell the story."

The girls, of course, were thrilled. Just before 12 o'clock that night, we crept quietly to the barn. (An hour earlier, I'd snuck out and plugged in a few small electric candles, so the stalls were bathed in a soft glow.)

Unnoticed, Tony slipped in the back door to start the tape, then caught up with us. "Now, remember, be quiet and carefully peek around the barn door," I warned the girls. "If the animals know we're here, they may be afraid to speak."

Just then, the tape began to play. A hush fell as our astonished daughters listened, hardly believing their ears.

Each Played a Part

The horses and ponies spoke of bringing supplies to the stable where the Christ Child was born. The donkey said he'd given Mary a ride when she was too tired to travel any farther.

The cows described bringing milk and cheese for Mary and Joseph, hungry after their journey, while the sheep bleated that they had offered a warm fleece for the Baby Jesus to sleep on.

The family dog boasted that he'd protected the little family after the Child was born and everyone had gone to sleep. Clucking hens proclaimed to be the first to hear angels' wings all around the stable.

The girls' pet kitties purred about how they kept the mice away and warmed Mary's feet as they curled up around her ankles. The rabbits were the last to speak, telling of gentle shepherds and a shining star.

The story done, an awed silence replaced it. We walked back to the house without exchanging a word. The girls didn't even mention Santa Claus—his visit had taken a backseat in all the excitement.

With their simple tale, the "animals" had supplied a powerful reminder of the true meaning of Christmas…one our children have never forgotten. ▲

Grandma's 'Brag' Page

WOULD THE *REAL* SANTA please stand up? Grandson Taylor plays St. Nick's spirited sidekick on Christmas Eve, relates Becky Rodgers from Rye, Colorado. With winning grin, he has no trouble filling holiday wishes for the whole family, she adds.

MOOOVE OVER, ST. NICK! Ryan Swendsen makes the cutest "Holstein Santa", pens proud Grandma Nancy Schroeder from dairy farm near Caledonia, Minnesota.

BEAR IN MIND... Proud Grandma Martha Frey enjoys sharing this picture-perfect shot of granddaughter Natashia flanked by a few festive furry friends. "It brings back such good holiday memories for me," Martha informs from her home at Forest, Ohio.

TRIPLE PLAY. Grandsons Rees, Zack and Garrett can't keep holiday spirit under their hats, writes Tyke McGuire, Etna, California. "It's a family tradition for the men to wear Santa caps Christmas Eve," she explains. "Even the littler guys like to join in."

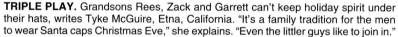

TIDINGS OF JOY. Grandchildren Laura, David, Sarah pose for Christmas card that reflects real reason for the season, remarks Linda Hathaway from Claypool, Indiana.

Santa Goes Modern

One day at the North Pole
Far, far away,
Santa was reading
The new *Toys for Today*.
"By jingles, I'll do it!"
He suddenly said.
"I'll write them a letter
Before going to bed."

"You...write a letter?
What on earth for?"
Mrs. Claus asked
As he went for the door.
"Mother," he said,
"These are new modern days.
There's simply no place
For our old-fashioned ways.

"A machine is in order,
One that makes toys
To help fill the orders
From good girls and boys."
The shop was soon filled
With machines bright and new
And Santa was reading
Just what he should do.

"Letters go here—
In this slot on the side.
The toys will come out
And run down this slide."
Tinsel brought letters
For Santa to try,
And Cranberry watched
As new toys slid by.

The elves took the toys
And put them away.
The job was all done
By the end of the day.
Later that night,
While Santa was sleeping,
It started in blowing
And snowing and sleeting.

Then down from the sky
Came a bright lightning bolt,
And it gave that machine
One terrible jolt.
When Santa came out
The next morning to work,
He turned on the switch...
Then pulled back with a jerk.

Sparks started flying—
Zing, *pop*, *bang*, *snap*—
And all of the letters
Were turned into scrap!
"The computer is ruined,
Burned out," Santa said.
"But at least there are toys
To pack in my sled."

"Oh, Santa," cried Tinsel
As he ran to his side,
"There's something the matter
With these toys I've tried.
The planes all fly backward,
The balls are like lead—
And the jack-in-the-box...
He falls out on his head!"

"What shall we do?"
Santa asked with a frown.
The elves started pacing
Around and around.
Just then Mrs. Claus
Came in with a treat.
"Mercy," she said
For the ruins at her feet.

"What's happened here
To our neat little shop?"
So Santa explained,
"The machine was a flop.
The letters are gone,
The toys are a mess.
There just won't be
Any Christmas, I guess."

"No Christmas? How silly,"
Mrs. Santa Claus said.
"You get that notion
Right out of your head!
Why, Nicholas, how many times
Have you told me,
Youngsters leave wish lists
Tucked under the tree?

"The elves should get busy
And make some new toys.
You'll know what to give
All the good girls and boys."
The air was soon filled
With laughter and singing.
The elves worked so fast
Their hammers were ringing.

The last toy was ready
Late Christmas Eve
As Santa got dressed up
And ready to leave.
But, first, he walked by
And said to each elf,
"There wouldn't be Christmas
If you hadn't helped!"

He got in his sleigh
And held the reins tight.
"Merry Christmas!" he called
As he drove out of sight.
Down each chimney he slid
With his pack full of gifts,
And he left what was asked
For on each child's list.

When at last he reached home
He took care of his sleigh,
Put his reindeer to bed
And gave each one some hay.
"You know, Dasher,"
He said as he gave him a pat,
"For Santa, the old way's
The best way at that!"

—Garness L. Russell
Corbin, Kentucky

The Memory Tree

A fiction story by Lori Jean Ness
Cambridge, Minnesota

"MOM," asked 13-year-old Lynda, clutching a child-sized rocking chair, "what happened to the big box of ornaments?" We were gathered in the family room to clear a space for the Christmas tree. And my heart ached at the answer I had to give to the four children staring at me expectantly.

"It went up in the attic after Dad took the tree down," I explained, trying to control my own emotions.

"You mean it got burned up?" Six-year-old Jon's eyes widened. "Just like my rocking horse and bug collection?"

Krista, our 3-year-old, burst into tears. "Hush, sweetie," I soothed. "It's okay. Mommy's here."

The ravenous fire that consumed our farmhouse 6 months earlier had also charred the edges of the children's security. They grieved again at each fresh reminder of a lost toy or treasured token of childhood.

"*We're* safe," I reminded them. "All we lost in the fire were things. Things can be replaced. People can't."

"So we're just gonna have a bare tree this year?" frowned 9-year-old David. "Won't it look kinda funny?"

"The tree won't be bare, silly!" Despite his confident tone, Jon turned to me for reassurance. "Will it, Mom?"

"No," I vowed. "I thought maybe we could take a trip to town on Saturday and buy some new ornaments."

"*Buy* them?" Lynda cried. "We can't just go to a store and replace that box!

"What about the reindeer Grandpa

carved when he was a boy? Or the snowflake Grandma helped me crochet when I was little? And that tiny green sled David painted when he was in second grade? We can't buy stuff like that!"

I rubbed the spot above my heart, trying to massage away the ache. Those ornaments had told the story of our family—how quickly they'd been reduced to ashes and soot.

"Now you made Mom cry!" Jon accused his big sister.

"Mom, I'm so sorry," Lynda apologized, chastened.

"It's okay, sweetheart. That box was filled with precious memories, but we can't dwell on what we don't have. Let's be glad we'll be together to celebrate Jesus' birthday. Now, no more blubbering, all right?"

We worked until bedtime. When I tucked in the children, I got some extra-big hugs.

"We have wonderful kids," I told my husband the next morning as we sipped our coffee. "Just call me blessed."

"If you say so—even though I was finally getting used to calling you Peggy." Doug dodged the piece of toast I tossed in his direction. He squeezed my hand as he headed outside to tackle the morning chores. "I know this is going to be a tough Christmas, honey," he said. "But we'll get through it,"

"Together we can do anything." I squeezed his hand back. The ache in my chest was still there, however.

Soon, it was the weekend. To my surprise, none of the children wanted to come on the Saturday shopping trip I'd promised. "We've got something more important to do," Lynda informed.

"A project!" Krista announced. She adored projects.

That afternoon—as I walked in the front door, arms loaded with grocery bags—I couldn't help picturing the twin milk cans from my grandfather's farm. They had flanked the entrance hall in our old house. During the holiday season,

they were always filled with evergreen branches, a woodsy scent greeting each visitor. I paused, missing them fiercely.

I blinked back tears. Then, to my surprise, I heard laughter in the family room. Following the happy sound to its source, I discovered Doug and the children—immersed in a sea of paper, ribbon, cloth, modeling clay and sequins.

"We're making memories!" Jon exclaimed, holding up a paper plate splashed with bright colors. "This is a picture of my birthday picnic in the pasture last summer. See, here's Uncle Matt and the bonfire…"

Krista tugged at my sleeve. "I drew a picture of my kitty. Daddy's gonna hang it on the tree with a silver ribbon."

"No store-bought ornaments for us, Mom. We're going to have a memory tree!" Lynda smiled radiantly. "Daddy helped us cut one from the woods, and we're making things to hang on it—things that remind us of happy times."

A proud evergreen stood in the corner, its branches already decked with a few misshapen ornaments. One of them was a crocheted snowflake.

Lynda noticed me gazing at it. "I made some mistakes," she whispered, "just like on the one Grandma and I crocheted together."

I hugged each of our children, then got down on the floor to make a few ornaments. The ache in my heart was gone—in its place, I felt a warm glow of peace.

Homemade memories, like cookies, truly are the sweetest!

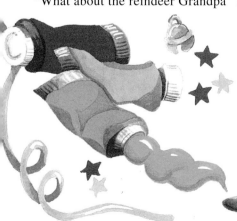

Craft Section...
Place Mats Make Sweet Table Treat

YOU'LL CREATE a feast for the eyes as well as the table when you complete these crafty Candy Cane Place Mats and Napkin Rings! Marion Kelley of Lansing, Michigan designed the colorful "cane-do" plastic canvas set as a quick and easy way to sweeten the season.

Materials Needed (for one place mat and one napkin ring):
Charts below and on next page
Two sheets of 7-mesh plastic canvas, 12 inches x 18 inches
Size 16 tapestry needle
Worsted-weight yarn—12 yards of red, 10 yards of green, 60 yards of white
Sharp craft scissors

Finished Size: Place mats are approximately 17 inches wide x 11 inches tall and napkin rings are 2-1/2 inches wide x 3 inches tall.

Directions:
Referring to charts, cut out the place mat and napkin ring shapes from plastic canvas, cutting pieces by counting bars and not holes. Also cut a 6-bar x 36-bar piece for the napkin ring band.

Using tapestry needle and 18-in. to 20-in. lengths of yarn, follow individual directions in next column to stitch place mat and two pieces for napkin ring.

Do not knot yarn on back of work. Instead, leave a 1-in. tail on the back of the canvas and catch it in the first few stitches. To end this yarn and begin the next,

run yarn ends under completed stitches on back of canvas, making sure to run under an area of matching color.

PLACE MAT: Use Continental and upright and slanted Gobelin stitches (Fig. 1) to fill in place mat as shown on chart, continuing established pattern across piece as directed.

Work upright Gobelin stitches over edge of piece to finish long top and bottom edges of place mat, then overcast remainder with colors shown on chart.

NAPKIN RING: Use Continental stitches to fill in napkin ring piece as

CANDY CANE PLACE MAT CHART (115 x 74 bars)

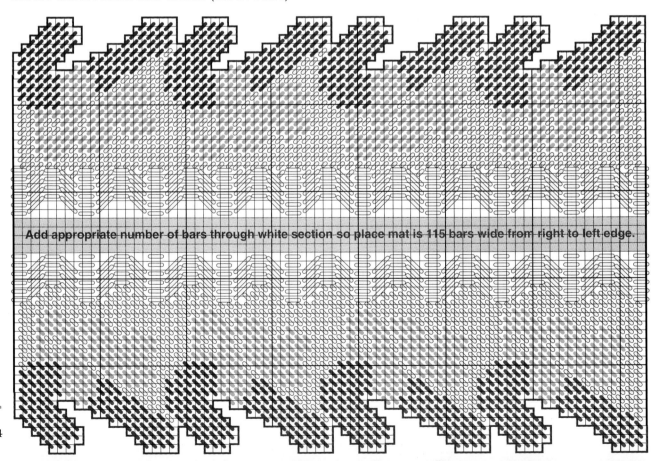

Add appropriate number of bars through white section so place mat is 115 bars wide from right to left edge.

Note: Continue white Gobelin stitches across center of place mat.

shown on chart. Overcast piece as shown.

Work center of band piece with slanted Gobelin stitches, then finish edges by working upright Gobelin stitches over the edge of the band piece as done for the place mat.

After both pieces have been worked, bring short ends of band piece together to form a circle and attach the ends of the band to the back of the stitches of the napkin ring piece.

Set your holiday table! ▲

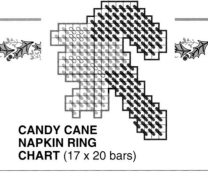

CANDY CANE PLACE MAT AND NAPKIN RING COLOR KEY
- ✎ Red
- ⊘ White
- ○ Green

OVERCAST-STITCHING
- — Red
- ▬ White
- — Green

Fig. 1

  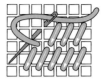

Upright Gobelin Stitch	Continental Stitch	Slanted Gobelin Stitch	Overcast Stitch

---

Son's Santa Is Doubly Crafty Claus

NO SPOOLING! You can put together this crafty Kris Kringle—designed by an inventive 11-year-old—in a flash.

When John Bush of Franklin, North Carolina surprised his mom, Ginger, with his Spool Santa at Christmas, she was properly impressed. "He knows I love handmade things," Ginger relates. "But I was even more pleased to find out he'd thought it up himself!"

John's spunky St. Nick can spread holiday cheer as either a gift topper or tree trimmer.

Materials Needed:
Pattern on this page*
Tracing paper
Pencil with new eraser
Red, black and yellow felt scraps
Empty thread spool, 2-1/4 inches high
Acrylic craft paints—red, black, white and flesh or peach
One cotton ball
1/2-inch white pom-pom
Paintbrush
Toothpick
Tacky (white) glue
Paper punch
Red thread
Standard sewing supplies

*Pattern and dimensions can be altered to fit different spool sizes.

Directions:
Trace hat pattern onto tracing paper and cut out piece for hat as directed on pattern. Also cut a 4-5/8-in. x 1/4-in. belt piece from yellow felt, a 4-5/8-in. x 7/8-in. coat piece from red felt and the "buttons" for Santa's coat, using a paper punch to punch two circles out of the black felt.

Paint the spool with peach or flesh paint, leaving the bottom edge unpainted. Let dry.

Paint bottom edge of the spool black and let dry.

Referring to photo at right, glue Santa's red coat around the bottom edge of the spool and his belt around the top edge of the coat, overlapping both at center back. Glue the black buttons down the front of the coat. Let dry.

Paint Santa's face as follows: Use the handle end of the brush to dot on black eyes and the eraser end of the pencil to dot on red cheeks. Let dry. Use the toothpick to add a white dot in the upper right side of each eye. Let dry.

Pull apart the cotton ball and glue a small piece of it onto Santa's chin to make the beard. Divide the remaining cotton into two pieces for the eyebrows. Glue both pieces on above Santa's eyes.

Match up the hat pieces and sew them together with a 1/8-in. seam, leaving bottom edge open. Trim the top point close. Turn the hat right side out and glue it to Santa's head.

Glue white pom-pom to the top of Santa's hat. ▲

SPOOL SANTA HAT
Cut 2—red felt

Leave open

55

Centerpiece Sets Shining Example for Bright Table

YOUR GUESTS will gladly see the light when you give this crafty candle holder a "starring" role at Yuletide get-togethers! Linda Whitener, a farm wife and elementary schoolteacher from Glen Allen, Missouri, came up with the bright idea for a brunch or buffet.

Materials Needed:

Patterns on next page
Tracing paper
Stylus or dry ballpoint pen
Transfer paper
Pencil
24 inches or scraps of 2 x 10 pine (actual size about 1-1/2 inches x 9-1/2 inches)
Scroll or band saw
Drill with 3/4-inch and 1/8-inch bits
12-inch length of 3/4-inch wooden dowel
Sandpaper
Paper towel
Acrylic paints—red and green
1-inch paintbrush
Satin spray finish
1-1/2-inch-tall x 1-1/4-inch-wide wooden candle cup
1-1/4-inch drywall screw
Screwdriver
6-inch red taper candle to fit in candle cup
Wood glue
Glass lamp globe, about 8-1/2 inches tall
Greenery and holly for wrapping around dowel

Finished Size: Candle holder (without glass globe) is 15-1/2 inches tall.

Directions:

Trace the star patterns onto tracing paper, completing each one as directed on pattern. Use transfer paper under patterns to transfer patterns onto the lumber with stylus or dry ballpoint pen, matching grainlines.

Cut out each star with scroll or band saw and sand the edges smooth, removing sanding dust with a damp paper towel. Drill a 3/4-inch hole all the way through the center of the medium star. Drill a 3/4-inch hole halfway through the center of the small star.

Paint the largest star, dowel and candle cup green. Paint the medium and small stars red. Let dry.

Glue the medium star on top of the large star, alternating the points as in Fig. 1. Let dry.

Drizzle glue in the hole of the small star and insert the dowel rod, pushing it in as far as it will go. Let dry.

Center candle cup on top of the small star and glue it into place. For added reinforcement, drill an 1/8-inch pilot hole through the candle cup into the small star and insert the drywall screw.

Spray a coat of finish on all sides of each piece. Let dry.

Place the dowel (with small star attached) into the hole in the medium star. You may glue this in place if you wish, or leave it unglued for easier storage.

Wrap the dowel with greenery and holly in an arrangement of your choice. Place the 6-inch taper candle in the candle cup and put the glass globe over the top of the candle.

Brighten up your holiday table! ▲

Fig. 1
Glue medium star to top of large star

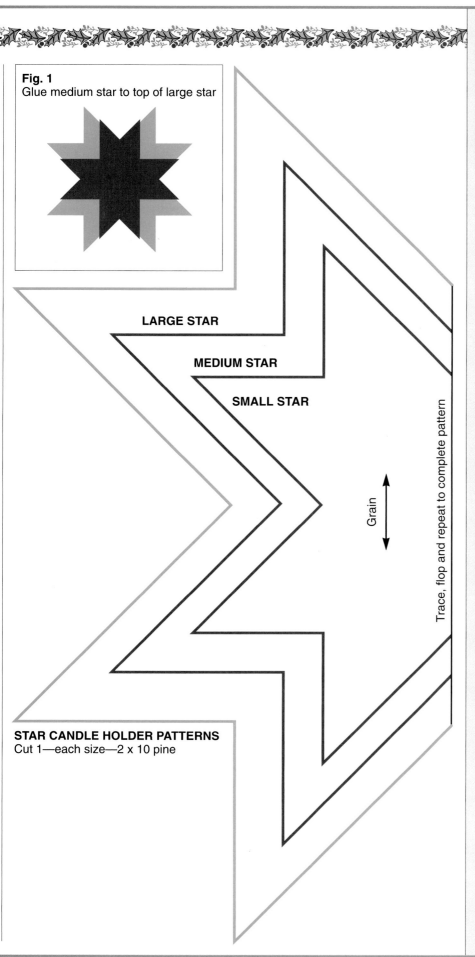

LARGE STAR

MEDIUM STAR

SMALL STAR

Grain

Trace, flop and repeat to complete pattern

STAR CANDLE HOLDER PATTERNS
Cut 1—each size—2 x 10 pine

Friends Craft a Sweet Exchange

WHEN restricted diets made a traditional Christmas cookie exchange too complicated for their group of a dozen, Vicki Maveus (above) and her friends turned crafty—and started an old-fashioned *ornament* exchange instead!

Over the past 14 years, this ambitious bunch from Sycamore, Illinois has gathered annually for a dinner at which more than *2,000* handmade ornaments have been swapped. "And we've never had a duplicate!" Vicki cheerfully advises. "We work hard to make our ornaments special and perfect."

The wide variety of techniques they employ ensures that each Yuletide crop is festively fresh. "Our decorations have been cross-stitched, ceramic, wooden, knitted, quilted, painted, papier-mache, beeswax, dough art...just about anything you can think of," Vicki notes.

Hostess duties are shared, with the women taking turns opening their homes and serving the entree. The rest of the group rounds out the merry meal with salads, side dishes and desserts.

Each tree trim that's exchanged comes with a unique yarn about its creation. "We laugh and cry over these stories," Vicki relates. "One friend had to dye the yarn for the ornament she was knitting. What a job that was! Another lady shared the story of the material she brought home from her trip to Scotland."

While they eagerly anticipate the eventful evening, she adds, December deadlines have a way of sneaking up. "We all say we'll be done by July each year. But come December, we're burning the midnight oil to finish our projects!"

As the years go by, these crafters are collecting more than just tiny bobs to beautify their boughs. "The party has helped deepen our friendships," Vicki observes. "When I decorate every year, I have wonderful memories of each person and her special creation." ▲

Creative Cards Come from Festive Fabrics

GIVE your holiday hellos a warm homespun touch with these crafty Christmas cards. An added benefit? They won't leave you pressed for time!

A cinch to make, according to designer Jan Koepsell of Paonia, Colorado, the cards require little more than scraps of material and your iron.

Materials Needed (for all three):
Patterns on next page
Blank cards (sold in stationery and art supply stores and card shops) or 12-1/2-inch x 4-5/8-inch piece of heavy paper (medium-weight watercolor paper, card stock or construction paper)
Matching envelopes
Pencil
Scraps of red and green cotton Christmas fabrics
Scraps of gold lamé fabric
Paper-backed fusible web
Iron

Press cloth or piece of muslin
Scissors
Fine-line permanent markers—black, brown and green

Finished Size: Each card is about 4-5/8 inches x 6-1/4 inches.

Directions:
If not using blank cards, fold 12-1/2-in. x 4-5/8-in. piece of paper in half crosswise for a 6-1/4-in. x 4-5/8-in. card.

Using patterns on next page, trace pattern pieces onto paper side of fusible web as directed on patterns. Cut out all shapes, leaving a small margin around each piece.

Preheat iron to medium (permanent press, no steam) setting. Place fusible-web shapes on wrong side of your fabric, using the following fabrics: your choice of Christmas prints for the ornament and wreath, contrasting Christmas prints for the bell and bow,

and gold lamé for the wreath bow and the ornament top. Press for 5 seconds to fuse. Let cool. Cut out pieces on traced lines and peel off paper backing.

Position pieces centered on each card, referring to photo above for placement and overlapping ornament top over ornament piece and bows over wreath and bell pieces. Touch each piece with the tip of the iron when it is positioned correctly to hold it in place while positioning other pieces. When all pieces are positioned correctly, cover the card with a press cloth or piece of muslin and press for 10 seconds to permanently fuse pieces in place.

To finish the ornament card: After fusing the ornament to the card, draw the evergreen branch using a brown marker. Draw the needles with a green marker and the loop from the top of the ornament to the branch with a black marker.

Sign your cards and send them on their way! ▲

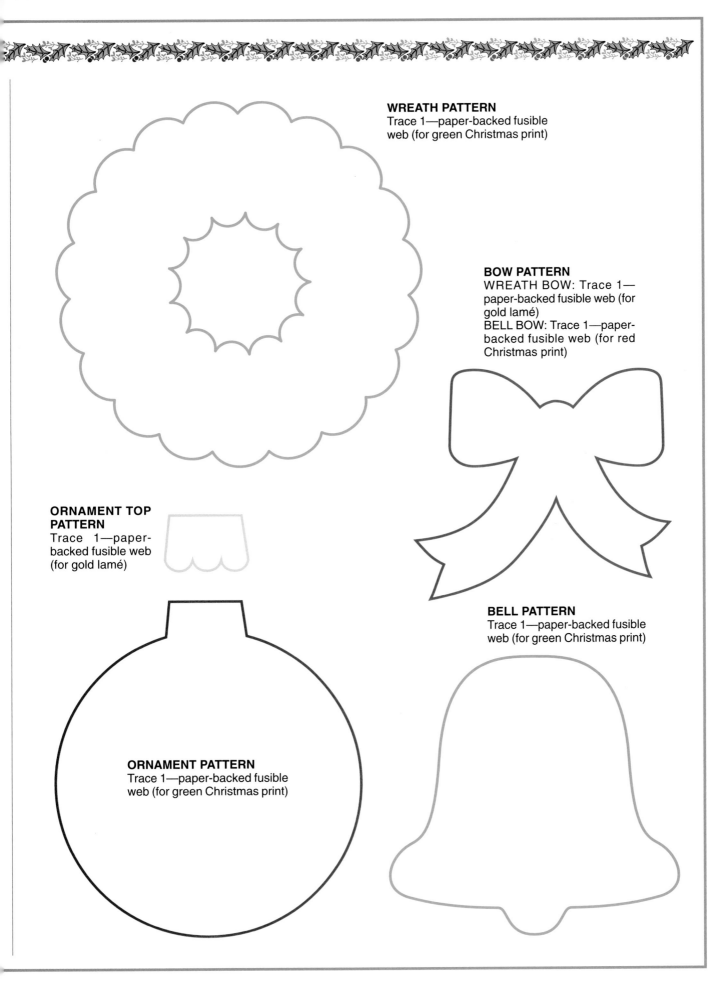

WREATH PATTERN
Trace 1—paper-backed fusible web (for green Christmas print)

BOW PATTERN
WREATH BOW: Trace 1—paper-backed fusible web (for gold lamé)
BELL BOW: Trace 1—paper-backed fusible web (for red Christmas print)

ORNAMENT TOP PATTERN
Trace 1—paper-backed fusible web (for gold lamé)

BELL PATTERN
Trace 1—paper-backed fusible web (for green Christmas print)

ORNAMENT PATTERN
Trace 1—paper-backed fusible web (for green Christmas print)

Pocket's Perfect Place to Gather Season's Greetings!

AT COLLECTING Christmas cards, this colorful country charmer's clearly a "star".

Jeanne Prue of Newport, Vermont, who fashioned the Feathered Star Card Holder, shares her time-saving secret for creating the quilted caddy—a shadow applique method!

The hanging holder has another useful side besides. Tuck a few candy canes in the flap, Jeanne explains, and you'll have a sweet server.

Materials Needed:
Patterns on next page
6-inch square of paper-backed fusible web
44-inch-wide 100% cotton fabrics
   —1/4 yard of white on white print, 1/8 yard of medium green print, 3/8 yard of dark green print, 1/2 yard of red solid and 3/8 yard of
any color for backing
1/4 yard of white tulle or fine bridal netting
10-inch x 16-1/2-inch piece of thin batting or fleece
8-1/2-inch piece of 1/4-inch dowel
Water-soluble fabric marker or quilt marker of your choice
Permanent marker
Quilter's ruler
Matching thread
White quilting thread
Quilting needle
Standard sewing supplies
Tracing paper
Pencil
Rotary cutter and cutting mat (optional)
Dowel for hanging

Finished Size: Card holder is approximately 9 inches wide x 15-1/2 inches high.

Directions:
Pre-wash, machine-dry and press all fabrics. Do all piecing with accurate 1/4-in. seams and right sides of fabric together. Press seams toward darker fabrics.

CUTTING: Cut squares and pieces using rotary cutter and quilter's ruler or scissors, pencil and quilter's ruler. Cut strips crosswise from selvage to selvage.

From white on white print, cut one 5-1/4-in. square and one 2-in. x 42-in. strip.

From medium green print, cut one 1-in. x 42-in. strip.

From dark green print, cut one 9-in. x 12-1/2-in. rectangle.

From red solid, cut one 9-in. x 7-in. rectangle for the pocket bottom. For the binding, cut one 1-1/2-in. x 12-in. strip and one 1-1/2-in. x 44-in. strip.

From backing fabric, cut one 10-in. x 16-1/2-in. piece.

From any leftover fabric, cut one 3-in. x 8-1/2-in. strip for the hanging sleeve.

From the tulle or bridal netting, cut one 9-in. square.

FEATHERED STAR SQUARE: Use a pencil to trace the patterns for the Feathered Star (A), eight diamonds (B) and octagon (C) onto the paper side of fusible web.

Leaving a margin around each piece, cut out around all shapes. Lay shapes fusible web side down on the wrong side of the appropriate fabrics as indicated with pattern. Fuse according to the manufacturer's directions.

Cut out the pieces on the lines marked. Remove paper backing.

Fold the 5-1/4-in. white on white print square into quarters diagonally and finger-press creases. Remove the paper backing from the fused pieces. Line up the Feathered Star so the outer spaces between the points line up with the creases. Fuse in place.

Referring to the photo at left, add octagon to center and add a diamond lined up with each point of Feathered Star. Fuse in place.

On the wrong side of the white on white print square, use a pencil to mark the midpoint of each side edge and the 1/4-in. seam line around the outer edge.

Stitch together the 42-in.-long medium green print and white on white print strips along one edge. Press and cut into four equal strips. Fold each strip in half and mark the midpoint of the long edge on each medium green print strip.

Line up a midpoint of a green print strip with each midpoint on the sides of the white on white print square. Pin in place with right sides together.

Stitch each side on the marked seam line, stopping and starting 1/4 in. from the raw edge at each corner. Press seams toward the green fabric.

To miter the corners, fold in half diagonally with right sides together and raw edges of borders even. Push the border seams up out of the way. Line up the 45° angle on the quilter's ruler with the raw edge of the border. With a pencil, draw a line from the corner of the inner square to the raw edge of the white on white print border (Fig. 1).

Pin and stitch on the drawn line, from the inner square to the outer edge of the border strips. Trim the seam to 1/4 in. and press to one side.

Layer tulle or bridal netting on top of bordered square. Baste around the outer edges.

Stitch the 9-in. x 7-in. red solid rectangle to one edge of border. Finger-press the seam toward the red solid fabric. *Be careful when pressing the tulle because it will melt at the "cotton" setting on your iron.*

QUILTING: Trace quilting design with permanent marker onto tracing paper. Place under each white border to trace design with water-soluble fabric marker.

On a table or mat, layer the backing wrong side up with the batting or fleece and top right side up. Pin and baste all around the outer edge and from center to corners, then horizontally and vertically through the Feathered Star de-

sign area and borders.

Quilt through all layers around each piece of the Feathered Star, next to the edge around both edges of the green border and on the marked border design. Trim backing and batting or fleece even with the top.

POCKET: Fold the 9-in. x 12-1/2-in. dark green print piece in half crosswise. Press. Baste pocket to top, lining up raw edges with bottom raw edges of red solid piece.

BINDING: Stitch the 1-1/2-in. red solid strips together at one short end, making one long strip.

Press the seam to one side. Press under 1/4 in. of one long edge of strip and one short end 1/4 in. to wrong side.

Begin with the short folded end to pin the strip to a side edge of the top, having right sides together, long folded edge out and raw edges even. Stitch through all layers, mitering corners as shown in Figs. 2a and b. Overlap at the end, trimming the red solid strip to overlap 1/2 in. beyond the beginning fold.

Fold the binding to the back of the piece, pinning edge to cover seam. Hand-sew the folded edge in place, mitering corners again. Remove all basting.

SLEEVE FOR HANGING: Turn under 1/4 in. at each end of the 3-in. x 8-1/2-in. strip. Press. Turn under 1/4 in. again and stitch.

Fold the strip in half lengthwise with *wrong* sides together and long edges even. Stitch the long edges together. Press the seam open, centering it on this side of the sleeve.

Position the sleeve just below the top binding with the seam side down on the back. Pin and hand-stitch the top and bottom edges to the back, being careful not to let the stitches go through to the front. Insert dowel to hang. ▲

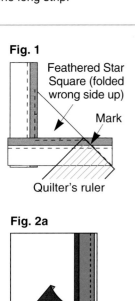

Fig. 1

Feathered Star Square (folded wrong side up)

Mark

Quilter's ruler

Fig. 2a

Stitch to 1/4 in. from corner and backstitch to corner

Fig. 2b

Form diagonal fold

Continue stitching

FEATHERED STAR PATTERNS
FEATHERED STAR (A): Trace 1—paper-backed fusible web (medium green print)
EIGHT DIAMONDS (B): Trace 8—paper-backed fusible web (red solid)
OCTAGON (C): Trace 1—paper-backed fusible web (red solid)

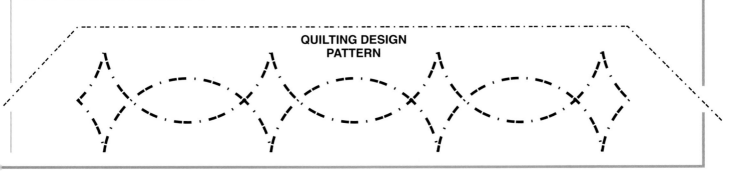

QUILTING DESIGN PATTERN

61

Her Door Decor Spreads Natural Holly-Day Cheer

DECK THE HALLS—or your doors or walls—with jolly holly when you make this winsome *wood* wreath. Pam Cecil of Keokuk, Iowa says it doesn't require much more than a few scraps of lumber, some jute and bright red beads to complete.

Materials Needed:

Pattern on next page
Tracing paper
Stylus or dry ballpoint pen
Transfer paper
Pencil
Scroll or band saw
3 feet of 1/4-inch x 10-inch pine
  lumber (or several small scraps)
One 18-inch or 20-inch grapevine
  wreath
Drill with 3/16-inch bit
Sandpaper
Acrylic craft paints—Bayberry, Calico
  Red, Thicket and Wrought Iron*
No. 6 flat paintbrush
Aleene's Glaze-It or other acrylic
  glazing finish
Small pieces of sponge for painting
19 yards of jute twine
Two yards of 3-1/2-inch-wide green
  paper twist
Spring-type clothespin
28 red 12mm round wooden beads
Scissors
Ruler
Vegetable oil (optional)
*Pam used Folk Art paints.

Finished Size: Wreath measures 18 to 20 inches in diameter.

Directions:

Trace leaf pattern onto tracing paper. Use transfer paper under pattern to transfer pattern 22 times onto the pine lumber with stylus or dry ballpoint pen, matching grainline.

Cut outside shape of each leaf with scroll or band saw. Drill a hole in each as indicated on pattern. Sand the edges smooth.

PAINTING: Leaves are painted with a series of washes, mixing paint with Glaze-It (or other glazing finish) for transparent color.

Mix a small amount of Bayberry paint with an equal amount of Glaze-It. Using a damp sponge, paint the front, back and sides of each leaf. Let dry.

Mix about 1 tablespoon of Glaze-It finish with 3-4 drops of Calico Red paint. Lightly apply mixture with sponge to the front of each leaf. Be sure to use only a small amount and always sponge in the direction of the grain. Let dry. (This should not cover the entire surface area, but simply be a highlight.)

Mix a small amount of Thicket paint with an equal amount of Glaze-It. Apply to leaves in the same way as the Calico Red, but more heavily on the leaf edges. Let dry.

Mix a small amount of Wrought Iron paint with an equal amount of Glaze-It. Using the flat brush, highlight the edges of the leaves and apply a streak down the center of each leaf. Let dry. (If desired, wipe a small amount of vegetable oil on the front of each leaf to make it shine.)

ASSEMBLY: Leaving a 4-in. space in the top center of the wreath, attach 11 leaves down each side. To do this, thread a 24-in. piece of jute through the hole in the top of the leaf.

Next, slip the jute under a twig or two of the wreath. Tie a double knot and thread a bead onto one end of the jute, pulling it all the way to the top of the leaf. Now tie a 2-1/2-in.-wide bow and trim the ends of the jute. Refer to photo above left for placement of the leaves, repeating this process for each leaf. The bottom third of the wreath should be left exposed.

BOW: To make the bow, untwist two 36-in. pieces of paper twist. Cut each piece in half lengthwise. Make two 4-in. loops in the center of each piece as in Fig. 1.

Stack the four looped pieces one on top of the other, using a clothespin to hold them in place.

Cut three 36-in. pieces of jute and make two 3-1/2-in. loops in the same manner as the paper twist pieces.

Use a 24-in. piece of jute to tie the centers of all the paper twist and the jute pieces together, knotting ends of jute together on the back of the bow and leaving the ends to attach it to the wreath.

Trim the paper twist bow ends at an angle fairly even with each other.

Trim the ends of the jute bow pieces at different lengths. String beads on the six jute ends and make a knot near each end to hold the beads in place. Tie the bow onto the top center of the wreath with the remainder of the 24-in. piece of jute. Hang up your wreath. ▲

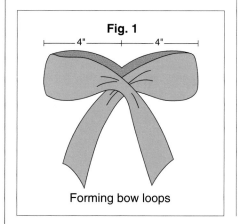

Fig. 1

4" 4"

Forming bow loops

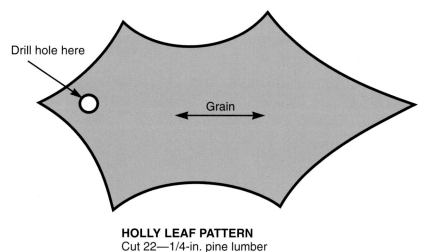

Drill hole here

Grain

HOLLY LEAF PATTERN
Cut 22—1/4-in. pine lumber

Ropes Add Zesty Yuletide Seasoning

HERE'S a decorating idea guaranteed to spice up your holiday kitchen. These braided baler twine ropes were a favorite of Sandra McKenzie, Braham, Minnesota, when she was a schoolgirl.

"Their spicy-sweet fragrance never failed to give me a warm holiday feeling," she recalls.

Now a farm wife, Sandra finds this project a festive way to recycle the twine from hay bales she feeds to her family's flock of sheep…while recycling some happy childhood memories as well!

If you're pining for your own supply of twine, a nearby farmer may be able to "bale" you out!

Materials Needed (for one spice rope):
Six pieces of baler twine, any color, each 48 to 60 inches long
Two pieces of baler twine, matching color, each 12 inches long
One 1-inch metal ring
Six pieces of beige yarn, each 8 inches long
Three cotton balls
Three 5-inch circles of Christmas print fabric
Three tablespoons of dried potpourri
Miniature painted pinecones or other holiday embellishments*
Cinnamon oil (optional)
Cotton swab
Glue gun and glue sticks
Scissors
Ruler

*You can use any type of embellishments to decorate your spice ropes (dried flowers, baby's breath, miniature candy canes, etc.). Sandra uses tiny pinecones she finds in the woods near her farm and sprays them with glitter or acrylic craft paint for an extra touch of color.

Directions:
BRAIDED TWINE: If using "recycled twine" from hay bales, trim off the knots before cutting pieces.

Pull the six pieces of 48-in. to 60-in. twine through the metal ring to the center of the pieces. Fold the pieces in half. To secure the twine on the ring, wrap a 12-in. piece of twine around the longer section of twine about 3/4 in. from the top. Tuck in ends and glue to back of piece.

Divide the longer twine pieces into three sections of four strands each and braid to approximately 1-1/2 ft. long. *(Hanging the ring on a nail makes braiding easier.)*

Using the other piece of foot-long twine, make another wrap at the bottom of the braid and glue ends in back.

Trim the braided twine to 2 in. below the second wrap. Untwist the ends of the braided twine to fray.

FABRIC BALLS: Place one cotton ball in each piece of Christmas fabric and surround it with 1 tablespoon of the dried potpourri. Gather edges together to form a fabric piece into a ball shape. Tie it close to stuffing, using an 8-in. piece of yarn. Use ends of piece to tie

ball to braided twine 1-1/2 in. below ring. Repeat with remaining fabric pieces, tying each to braided twine as shown in photo below.

Tie another piece of yarn around braid and ball together, forming a bow in front of each.

Glue on pinecones or other small embellishments between fabric balls as shown in photo.

Dip the cotton swab in the cinnamon oil and brush it on the bottom of each fabric ball if desired. ▲

2-inch square of heavy plastic or
  cardboard
Waxed paper
Burnt umber oil paint
Brush cleaner or paint thinner
Newspapers
Old toothbrush
Walnut wood stain
36 inches of 19-gauge black-finished
  (dark annealed) wire
3/4-inch gold jingle bell
Matte spray finish

*Patricia used DecoArt Americana
acrylic craft paint in Snow White, Santa
Red, Medium Flesh, Antique White, Glo-
rious Gold and Black.

Finished Size: Santa wall hanging is
about 7 inches wide x 15 inches tall.

Directions:
Trace patterns onto tracing paper, completing Santa pattern as directed on pattern. Use transfer paper under patterns
to transfer them onto wood (Santa to 1 x
8 pine; hearts to 1/4-in.-thick wood) using a stylus or dry ballpoint pen and
matching grainlines.

Cut outside shape of each piece with
a scroll or band saw. Drill holes in Santa, hearts and star as shown on patterns.

Sand each piece on all sides until
smooth. Remove sanding dust with tack
cloth.

PAINTING: Transfer outline of Santa's face, fur trim and pom-pom on his
hat to Santa piece.

Using the No. 8 flat brush, basecoat
front and edges of cut pieces as follows:
beard and mustache with black, the fur
trim and pom-pom on hat with antique
white, the hat and hearts with red and
the face with flesh. Basecoat the star
cutout using No. 4 round brush and gold
paint. It may take more than one coat to
cover each piece. Let dry between coats.

Stenciling: Transfer the star pattern
and cheek circles to the 2-in. square of
heavy plastic or cardboard. Cut them out
to make stencils using the craft (X-Acto)
knife.

Using the stencil brush, stencil the
cheek circles on Santa's face and stars
on the hearts. Referring to patterns,
place appropriate stencil in position on
wood piece. Dip stencil brush in paint
and wipe off on paper towel so it is almost dry. Hold brush perpendicular to
piece and lightly apply paint with an up-
and-down motion in cutout area, using
red paint for cheeks on Santa and gold
paint for stars on hearts. Let dry.

Details: Paint the words freehand on
the hearts or transfer the patterns, then
use the No. 1 liner brush and antique

Wooden Santa's Full of Lively Old-Styled Fun

LET this seasoned Santa "hang around"
your place and you're sure to have a
popular fellow on your hands. "He's
one of my best-sellers at holiday craft
shows," notes crafter Patricia Schroedl
of Jefferson, Wisconsin, who mixed a
palette of paints and festive finishes to
create his uniquely antique look.

Materials Needed:
Patterns on next page
Tracing paper
Transfer paper
Stylus or dry ballpoint pen
12-inch piece of 1 x 8 pine lumber
  (actual size about 3/4 inch x
  7-1/2 inches)
3-inch x 5-inch piece of 1/4-inch-thick
  wood
1-inch wood star cutout
Scroll or band saw
Drill with 1/16-inch bit
Sandpaper
Tack cloth
Acrylic craft paint—white, red, flesh,
  antique white, gold and black*
DecoArt Weathered Wood (or other
  crackle medium)
Palette or paper plate
Paintbrushes—No. 8 flat, No. 1 liner,
  No. 4 round, 1/4-inch stencil and
  1-inch sponge brush
Toothpick (optional)
Paper towels
Craft (X-Acto) knife

white paint to paint the straight lines and a stylus or toothpick to dot the ends of the letters.

Using the handle end of a large brush, make 1/4-in. dots for Santa's eyes with black paint. Let dry. Use the stylus or toothpick and white paint to make one small dot in the upper right corner of each eye for highlight.

Use the No. 4 round brush and white paint to paint Santa's eyebrows.

Shade the nose and lip with red paint and the No. 8 flat brush. To shade, dip the paintbrush in clean water. Remove excess water by touching the brush to a paper towel until the shine disappears. Gently touch one corner of the brush in red paint and brush it back and forth on waxed paper to blend the paint into the brush. Apply the paint with the loaded edge of the brush toward line marked on pattern.

Use the handle end of a large brush to apply dots of white paint on the fur trim and pom-pom of Santa's hat, applying the dots so they fill the front and side edges of these areas.

Apply the Weathered Wood or crackle finish to Santa's beard and mustache, covering the front and side edges of these areas. Let dry.

Using the No. 8 flat brush, stroke white paint over the beard and mustache, covering the front and side edges. Let dry.

Apply burnt umber oil paint, thinned with brush cleaner, all over Santa and the hearts using the sponge brush. Wipe off excess with paper towels. Let dry.

To spatter the wood pieces, thin a small amount of gold paint with water until it is the consistency of ink. Cover your work area with newspaper and place Santa and the hearts on the paper. Dip the old toothbrush in gold paint. Hold the toothbrush 6 in. in front of the wood pieces. Pull any other paintbrush handle toward you over toothbrush bristles to spatter the wood pieces. Repeat the process until you achieve the desired effect.

FINISHING: Referring to pattern, use craft (X-Acto) knife to carve along lines around the face, mustache, fur trim, and pom-pom on hat. Whittle some wood from the edges all around the beard and hat.

Stain front, back and edges of Santa with wood stain. Let dry.

Insert wire through hole in Santa's pom-pom and pull about 3 in. of wire above the hat. Bring both ends of wire together and twist together. Bend longer end down 4 in. above Santa and twist it together, leaving a 1-1/2-in. loop for hanging as in Fig. 1. Thread the "I Believe" heart onto wire 3-1/2 in. below hanging loop. Make a loop in the wire, twisting wire once above heart to hold it in place. Repeat the process with "In Santa" heart about 3 in. below first heart.

Thread the star cutout and the jingle bell onto the wire about 3 in. below the second heart. Loop and twist the wire to hold them in place. Wrap the remaining end of the wire around a pencil or brush handle to form a curl.

Spray the entire piece with matte spray finish. Let dry. ▲

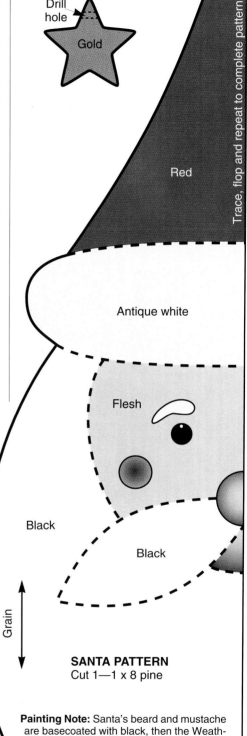

STAR DRILLING PATTERN

Drill hole — Gold

Drill hole — Antique white

Red

Trace, flop and repeat to complete pattern

Antique white

Flesh

Black

Black

Grain

SANTA PATTERN
Cut 1—1 x 8 pine

Painting Note: Santa's beard and mustache are basecoated with black, then the Weathered Wood or crackle finish is applied and they are painted white. (Allow time to dry between coats.) The Weathered Wood or crackle finish cracks so the black basecoat shows in the cracks throughout the white beard and mustache.

Fig. 1
Adding wire

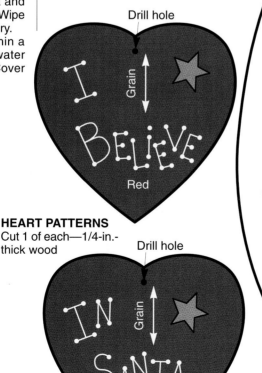

Drill hole

I BELIEVE
Grain
Red

HEART PATTERNS
Cut 1 of each—1/4-in.-thick wood

Drill hole

IN SANTA
Grain
Red

Banner's Brimming Bright With Scraps of the Season

CHRISTMAS comes together from all over in this quilted wall hanging pieced together from a potpourri of pretty and festive fabrics.

Susan Weakley, a seasoned seamstress from Lake Leelanau, Michigan, crafted the scrappy stocking to deck her walls. She's also given one to friends as an extra-special gift.

Hang this stocking by the chimney with care and it's sure to be a bright spot in *your* holidays, too.

Materials Needed:
Pattern on next page
Tracing or pattern paper
Pencil
44-inch-wide 100% cotton fabrics—
 1 yard of white on white print,
 1/2 yard of red solid, 1/4 yard each
 of red pin dot, red/white stripe and
Christmas print of choice
Scraps of Christmas prints (for stocking)
3/4 yard of any fabric for backing and
 hanging sleeve
22-inch square of lightweight batting
One 6-inch square of muslin (for base of
 crazy-quilting)
White and red thread
White hand-quilting thread
Water-erasable marker
Quilter's ruler
Rotary cutter and cutting mat (optional)
Standard sewing supplies

Finished Size: Wall hanging is about 19 inches x 20 inches.

Directions:
Pre-wash fabrics without fabric softeners, washing colors separately. If the water from the red fabrics is discolored, wash again until rinse water runs clear. Dry and press all fabrics.

Use accurate 1/4-in. seams with right sides of fabric together. Press seams toward darker fabrics when possible.

CRAZY-QUILTING: Trace stocking pattern onto tracing or pattern paper and cut out pattern. Trace around stocking pattern onto 6-in. muslin square using water-erasable marker. Also trace 1/2 in. outside of stocking pattern outline.

Cut varying-width strips or uneven pieces of your fabrics, making sure all edges are straight. Pin the first piece right side up on the left side of the heart as in Fig. 1a. Place the next fabric to be used wrong side up over the first piece and machine-stitch through all layers in a 1/4-in. seam as in Fig. 1b. Flip the second piece up, cutting to shape if desired. Pin edges in place.

Continue adding pieces as in Fig. 1c, sewing with right sides together, flipping and cutting to shape, then pinning in place until the entire larger stocking shape (1/2 in. beyond original pattern) is covered with pieces of fabric.

Trace stocking pattern again onto crazy-quilted piece, choosing your favorite section of the piece. Cut stocking out on traced line.

CUTTING: Accurately cut pieces, squares and strips using rotary cutter and quilter's ruler or scissors, water-soluble or quilt marker and ruler, cutting strips crosswise from selvage to selvage.

From white on white print, cut one 8-1/2-in. x 9-1/4-in. piece (center background) and eleven 1-1/4-in. x 14-in. strips. From red solid, cut eleven 1-1/4-in. x 14-in. strips, two 2-1/4-in. x 44-in. strips and four 2-1/2-in. squares. From red pin dot, cut one 1-1/2-in. x 44-in. strip. From red/white stripe, cut two 1-in. x 44-in. strips (or cut four 1-in. x 12-in. strips on the bias if desired). From Christmas print, cut two 2-1/2-in. x 44-in. strips. From backing fabric, cut a 22-in. square for backing and a 4-1/2-in. x 19-in. strip for optional hanging sleeve.

APPLIQUEING: Press under 1/4 in. on all edges of crazy-quilted stocking piece, clipping to fold on curve. Pin to center of 8-1/2-in. x 9-1/4-in. white on white print piece. Hand-stitch edges in place with matching thread.

ASSEMBLING: Borders: Stitch one end of the 1-1/2-in. x 44-in. red pin dot strip to one side of the appliqued center piece. Press seam toward strips. Trim ends even with edges of center piece. Repeat, adding strip to opposite side of center piece. Repeat for top and bottom, trimming strips even with edges of side strips.

Repeat to add a border of the 1-in. red/white stripe strips, then a border of the 2-1/2-in. Christmas print strips to

complete wall hanging top.

Checked Border: Join 10 of the 1-1/4-in. x 14-in. red solid strips with 10 of the 1-1/4-in. x 14-in. white on white strips to form a set of strips as shown in Fig. 2a. Press. Cut the set of strips into eight 1-1/2-in. pieces. (Extra length has been allowed on these strips.) Also cut two 1-1/2-in. pieces from each remaining 1-1/4-in. strip.

Stitch the 1-1/2-in. sets and pieces together in pairs as shown in Fig. 2b. Press. Add a 20-piece set to the top and bottom of the wall hanging top. Press.

Add a one-piece set to the end of two of the 20-piece sets for the side borders. Stitch one of these 21-piece sets to each side of wall hanging top. Press seam toward Christmas print border.

Add a 2-1/2-in. red solid square to each end of the remaining 20-piece sets and stitch to top and bottom of wall hanging top, matching seams of square to seams of 21-piece sets. Press.

BACKING: Place the 22-in. backing square wrong side up on a flat surface and smooth out wrinkles. Place batting over backing and smooth out. Center wall hanging top over batting, right side up, again smoothing out wrinkles.

QUILTING: Pin, then baste through all layers, stitching from center to corners, then horizontally and vertically every 4 in. until entire top is held together.

"Echo-quilt" around stocking, using white quilting thread to stitch first quilting line 1/4 in. away from stocking. Add next stitching line 1/4 in. outside of first. Continue adding lines 1/4 in. outside of previous one until six are completed.

Machine-quilt with white thread, stitching-in-the-ditch at the edge of the center block and both edges of the Christmas print border.

Hand-quilt a white "X" in the four red solid corner blocks. Remove basting stitches. Trim backing and batting even with edges of wall hanging top.

BINDING: Stitch short ends of the two 2-1/4-in. x 44-in. red solid binding strips together to make one long strip. Fold strip in half lengthwise and press. With raw edges of strip matching raw edges of wall hanging, sew binding to front, mitering corners. Fold binding to back of wall hanging and hand-stitch folded edge in place over seam.

HANGING SLEEVE (optional): Finish the short ends of the 4-1/2-in. x 19-in. white solid hanging sleeve piece by folding under 1/4 in. twice and edge-stitching inside fold.

Folding wrong sides and raw edges together, stitch long edges together to make a tube. Press seam open and center it on one side.

Pin seam side against top back of wall hanging with upper edge just below binding. Hand-stitch along long folds and part of hemmed ends that lie against back. ▲

Fig. 1a
Crazy-quilting

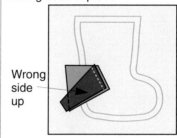

Right side of first piece

Muslin

Fig. 1b
Adding second piece

Wrong side up

Fig. 1c
Adding third piece

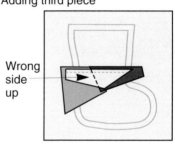

Wrong side up

1/4-in. seam allowance

Clip

STOCKING APPLIQUE PATTERN

Fig. 2a
Checked border

1-1/2 in.
1-1/2 in.
1-1/2 in.

Cut 8

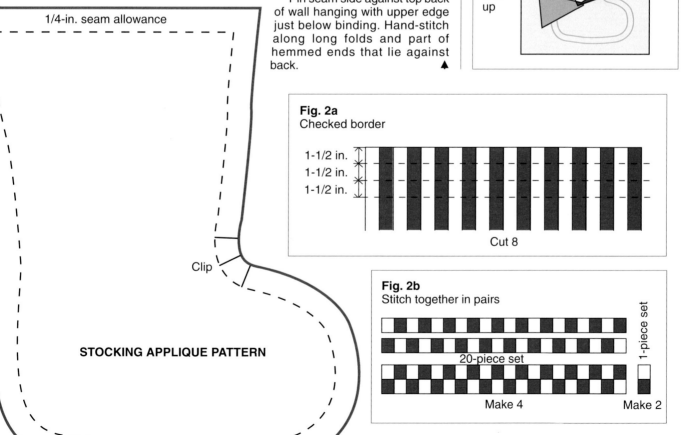

Fig. 2b
Stitch together in pairs

20-piece set

1-piece set

Make 4   Make 2

Her Berry Basket Conveys Very Merry Holiday Feeling

IS your strawberry basket gathering dust waiting for next summer's crop? Consider using it to spread the spirit of the season instead!

By following the simple instructions below from Christine Ballentine of Attica, Michigan, you can turn your basket into a charming Christmas catchall …or fill it to the brim with homemade bounty to share the fruits of your labors.

Materials Needed:
Berry basket, 5 x 5 x 3-1/4 inches
1-3/4 yards of 4-inch-wide paper twist, in red, white or green
1/4 yard of Christmas print fabric for basket lining
Paper towels
2/3 yard of beading lace with ribbon inserted, having 1-1/4-inch pregathered lace sewn to one edge, plus 2 yards of 1/4-inch double-face satin ribbon (both to match either paper twist or lining fabric)
One or two small Christmas decorations, such as holly berries, miniature ornaments, etc.
Glue gun and glue sticks
12 large paper clips or spring-type clothespins

Directions:
Cut three 13-in. pieces of paper twist. Untwist all pieces and cut in half lengthwise to form six bottom strips. Cut one 22-in. piece, untwist, then cut in thirds lengthwise, making three strips, each about 1-1/4 in. wide.

BASKET BOTTOM: Place three bottom strips parallel to each other on a flat surface with wrong side of paper twist up. Weave remaining three strips wrong side up through the first strips by alternating under then over with each piece as in Fig. 1, forming a 4-1/2-in.-square bottom.

Center basket on top of woven bottom. Pull ends of each strip up and over basket edge, securing with paper clips or clothespins.

BASKET SIDES: Remove the clothespin from one of the center strips of paper twist and fold it down. Glue one of the 22-in. side strips (right side out) to the lower edge of the basket under loosened strip and weave horizontally over and under strips around the basket, removing and replacing paper clips as you work around the basket. Trim off excess on side strip, allowing 1/2 in. to overlap. Glue ends together behind loosened strip. (See Fig. 2.)

Turn basket a quarter turn and repeat with next side strip. Turn again and weave final side strip.

Glue ends of paper twist to inside of basket, stretching or easing-in strips to cover top edge of basket side completely.

BASKET LINING: Cut two 12-in. x 6-1/2-in. pieces of lining fabric.

Hold two pieces of paper towel together. Fold them in thirds to make a piece about 10 in. long x 4-1/4 in. wide. Center on wrong side of one piece of lining fabric, folding and gluing edges of fabric to paper towel to make a 10-in. x 5-in. piece. Repeat for second piece.

Place one lining piece right side up in the basket, having short ends even with opposite top edges of basket. Glue short ends of lining to inside top edge of basket. Repeat with remaining piece, gluing it to the opposite sides of the basket.

FINISHING: Beginning in the center of any side of the basket, glue lace beading along upper edge. Overlap ends 1/2 in. and trim.

Cut a 6-in. piece of ribbon. Form a bow by winding remaining ribbon loosely around your hand to make about five 3-1/2-in. loops. Tie center with 6-in. piece of ribbon and glue bow over lace ends. Glue one or more small decorations below bow.

Fill your basket with wrapped cookies or candy for a special Christmas gift. Or fill it with scented pinecones, Christmas soaps, etc. and decorate your house with it. ▲

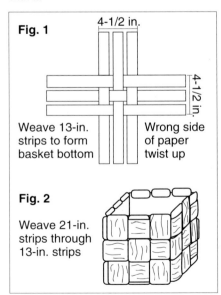

Fig. 1

4-1/2 in.

4-1/2 in.

Weave 13-in. strips to form basket bottom

Wrong side of paper twist up

Fig. 2

Weave 21-in. strips through 13-in. strips

Farm Full of Christmas Features Festive Crop

By D. Wilson of Beaverton, Oregon

THERE'S no hiding it! "I'm in love," glows Betty McCready, "with Christmas."

All the same, when she and husband Tom built a 60-foot-long barn on their Sherwood, Oregon tree farm—Pacific Christmas Trees—Betty never dreamed it would grow into the largest Christmas shop in the area.

"During our first year offering trees," she recalls, "we had cookies and hot chocolate available in the barn. Soon, customers were suggesting it would make a perfect shop."

Daughter Molly came up with a festively fitting name, and Sleighbells blossomed in 1985. It's flourished ever since.

These days, a huge variety of tree trimmers and handmade holiday decorations packs its 6,000 square feet. "First-time visitors are amazed at all there is," Betty chuckles. "The looks on their faces make me so happy."

Besides a big selection of Christmas collectibles, Sleighbells features the work of local crafters who create wood

carvings, hand-knitted stockings, angels, tole paintings, tree skirts and more. "I like to offer things that may not be available elsewhere," Betty notes.

Sleighbells is a family-friendly shop with plenty of items for men and children's stocking stuffers. For instance, figurines and ornaments geared to hunters, fishermen and outdoor enthusiasts are staples.

It's family-friendly in another way as well. Son David and daughter-in-law Annette assist with bookkeeping and promotions. Meanwhile, niece Carrie operates the snack bar.

To help shoppers enjoy a "well-rounded" visit, Betty opened the Wreath House next door. There, well-known perennial grower Margaret Willoughby offers her handcrafted dried flower wreaths and arrangements. She also teaches her techniques to groups using the barn's meeting rooms.

As an added treat, shoppers can visit the "North Pole"—the gazebo-shaped observatory overlooking the farm—for a breathtaking peek at Mount Hood.

And, even after the peak of holiday activity has passed, Betty and her crafty crew don't rest. "Come January, we're eagerly back to preparing for the *next* season," she informs. "We're so happy to offer a farm full of Christmas!"

Editor's Note: *Sleighbells Christmas Shop and Pacific Christmas Trees are open daily 10 a.m.-5 p.m. June 1 through the end of December. The Wreath House is open October 15 until mid-December. For more information, contact Sleighbells, 23855 S.W. 195th Pl., Sherwood OR 97140; 1-800/809-8784.* ▲

RINGING IN the season with good cheer is Betty McCready (above), who stocks festive shop on family tree farm with crafty Christmas creations—tree skirts, jolly Santas, sweet treats, more!

Readers' Poetry Corner

Hodgepodge Tree

Designer trees are beautiful,
A wonder to behold—
All draped in patchwork, crimson birds,
In silver bells or gold.

But I'm a sentimental soul;
I thrive on memory.
Each ornament is hung with love
Upon my hodgepodge tree.

The crooked star upon the top
Is one my daughter made
Of beads she strung on floral wire
When she was in third grade.

The toothpick snowflakes, painted cones
Are treasures dear to me.
My youngest son helped fashion them
When he was only three.

A clothespin angel, bread dough wreath,
Imperfect handmade art—
Each thing recalls a Christmas past
That's special to my heart.
—Louise Pugh Corder
Franklinville, North Carolina

Christmas Snow

The Christmas snow worked magic
As it fell all through the night
And made a world of wonder
So pure and soft and white.
The backyard's cloaked in ermine
With a little pine corsage,
And the mountain in the front yard
Is really the garage.
I'm glad old Santa made it
Before the roads were closed…
Since now we'll all be housebound
Until the lane is 'dozed!
—Bess Michael
La Jose, Pennsylvania

OH CHRISTMAS TREE is timely tune year-round at the cheerful tree farm of Donna Slusher (above left). Donna and daughter Krystal spruce up family's homegrown favorite (below right).

Grower's on Cutting Edge Of Happy Holiday Harvest

ANY NUMBER of country women start preparing for the Christmas season early. Few can compare with Donna Slusher, however. Her holiday head start stretches for a full 7 years!

That's how long it takes the seedlings on her family's Lexington, Missouri Christmas tree farm—Lumber Jack's—to mature…and make another family's holidays extra special.

Donna's a natural at helping customers pick the perfect pine. "As a child," she smiles, "I always looked forward to getting our Christmas tree. I appointed myself the official decorator. Today, my husband, Scott, and our girls—Megan, 10, Tiffany, 8, and Krystal, 5—say I still hold the title!"

Christmas trees are part of Donna's life all year. Early spring finds her, planting bar in hand, setting out the seedlings. Summer means "mowing, mowing and more mowing". Come fall, she's a frequent speaker at local clubs with her festive flair for wreath and bow making.

The reward for all that effort comes in late November when the farm opens to the public. "It's fun helping new friends choose the ideal tree," Donna observes. "But the greatest pleasure is greeting returning families year after year. We have watched many of our customers grow up before our eyes."

Right along with their Christmas trees, she might add.

Editor's Note: *Lumber Jack's Christmas Tree Farm is open the Friday after Thanksgiving through Christmas Eve. Hours are Friday through Sunday from 10 a.m. to dusk or by appointment. For information or a price list, contact Lumber Jack's, Rt. 2, Box 108, Lexington MO 34057; 1-816/259-6428.*

'Pro' Shares Secrets to *Perfect* Christmas Tree

ACCORDING to Donna Slusher, there are several keys to being happy all holiday season with the Christmas tree you choose:

● Make sure the trunk is straight and remember to check the size of the tree's base. "They'll be important considerations when you put the tree in your stand," she advises.

● Check to see if there are open areas on the tree that detract from its appearance.

● Depending on the weights and types of ornaments you display, also look at the tree's branching angle.

● "Most importantly," Donna concludes, "go with what you like!" ▲

I'll Never Forget...

Waiting for Christmas To Come Round Left Curious Children Stuck

By Laura Martin-Palmatier of Binghamton, New York

Which one of my childhood Christmases was the most memorable? I don't have any trouble "fingering" it.

In December 1945, I was 9…my twin sisters—Bev and Bea—were 12…and we were about to discover just how tight a tight squeeze could be.

The worst of winter came early that year. Our isolated farm sat at the top of a hill, and the wind often blew the snow across the road into deep impassable drifts. Sometimes, we'd have to wait for days to get plowed out.

Early Arrivals

Our grown sisters, who normally came home to celebrate the holidays, started to worry that a storm might prevent them from making the trip. So they mailed our presents, just in case. Then a cousin did the same. Before we knew it, there was a blizzard of gifts under our tree!

Today, the presents we received—coloring books and crayons, card games and puzzles, diaries with keys, writing paper, costume jewelry, socks and dainty linen hankies—would be considered stocking stuffers. To us, though, they were mysterious treasures…treasures that grew more tempting with each passing day.

Mother noticed our longing glances at the secret bounty beneath the tree. Every night, as she lit the lantern and started out to the barn to help with milking, she reminded us to be patient, that the mounting pile of presents was intended for opening on Christmas Day.

Night after night, we were obedient angels—until the evening we decided we'd peek at *one* present. "We'll just look in that odd-shaped box that doesn't rattle when you shake it," we told ourselves, truly planning to leave it at that.

Just One Look?

We did…at least, *that* particular night. Come the following ones, however, our curiosity spun out of control. Soon, we were examining the contents of *every* package—even inspecting our father's plaid flannel shirts and mother's thread holder!

Like cracking a safe, opening those packages was a delicate process that couldn't be hurried. (There were no stick-on bows back then, and ribbons were tied tightly around presents.) So we dared peek at but a few gifts each night.

As the big day drew closer, more gifts arrived from our sister Dot. Hers were covered with warning stickers, "Do Not Open Until Christmas!"

That evening, sister Bev struck gold when the tiny package she pried open contained the beautiful ring she'd been fervently hoping for. She slipped it on her finger for a moment and admired the way it glistened in the lamplight. Then it was time to rewrap the ring.

Bev tried to slide it off her finger—but it wouldn't budge.

"Come on!" Bea and I prodded her. "Hurry up!"

Bev put her finger in her mouth and gripped the ring tightly with her teeth. She pulled *hard*. Still, the ring wouldn't move at all.

No Soap!

By now, Bev's finger was turning red and starting to swell. Desperate measures seemed called for! We rubbed

> *"We were obedient angels —'til we decided to peek at just one present…"*

her finger with lard…to no avail. We tried soap. No luck.

The clock was ticking. Any minute, we'd spot the orange glow of Mother's lantern as she walked back from the barn. We had to do *something*.

Just in time, Bea had a brainstorm. Without a word, she grabbed a cup and raced outside. When she returned, she was carrying a cupful of new-fallen snow…into which she immediately plunged Bev's finger.

Oh, that snow was cold! It was also *very* effective, however, in subduing our sister's stubborn swelling. When, at last, we allowed Bev to take her poor half-frozen finger out of the cup, all that was required was a small application of soap. Miracle of miracles, the ring slipped right off!

We got it wrapped up and hidden back under the tree just a few footsteps ahead of Mother. If she suspected anything, she never let on. As for us, after that unforgettable experience, we *never* touched another gift before Christmas! ▲

Homespun Santas Highlight the Season

Perching on a shelf...trimming the tree...or greeting guests on the porch, Santa's always afoot at holiday time. In that spirit, crafters from coast to coast create a festive flurry of Clauses.

PILLAR TO POST. Fence-post Santa Marsha Kasner of Foley, Minnesota made is an outdoorsy type—with tree-branch arms and belt buckle fashioned from an old door latch.

IN WITH THE OLD. Papier-mache Santas get antique outlook from pair of Linda Hilbert, Joan Spence. Crafty business grew from holiday hobby, they write from Cincinnati, Ohio.

DON'T POUT! Family names painted on elf's "nice list" by grandma make ceramic St. Nick keeper for Monique Teeple, Anola, Manitoba.

IT'S ALL IN THE FAMILY at Lansing, Illinois crafter Patti Cherney's home. Jolly old elves of yarn and felt branch out on the tree.

PANTA CLAUS. Anita Noland, Alva, Oklahoma, treasures sister's handiwork—St. Nick stitched from their grandpa's striped overalls.

Holiday Open House Has History on Display, Too

WISHING for new furniture for Christmas? Jan Richenburg's just the opposite. She's excited to see *old* furniture arriving in time for the holidays at her Salisbury, Massachusetts farmhouse!

Jan's family has worked Pettengill Farm for more than 200 years...and, each November, she likes to share its history through an annual weekend open house.

"We completely remove our normal furnishings from the first floor," she notes. "Then a local antique dealer brings in period furniture to temporarily take its place."

When Jan was growing up on the 100-acre farm, her father grew vegetables and sold them at a small roadside stand. These days, with Jan and husband Henry at the helm, it's fresh and dried flowers that are the farm's cheerful crops.

"The open house, though, is the biggest project we do," she advises. "Our home has some beautiful old features we wanted to let others see."

With the "new" antique furniture in place, Jan cultivates her own holiday look with wreaths, bouquets, baskets, swags, mantel and table arrangements, and more—crafted with dried flowers and herbs, grapevines, raffia or even fresh fruit!

"We decorate *all* the rooms," she points out. "Each has its own Christmas tree with color-coordinated ornaments, most of which we've homemade."

It takes a crew of 27 eager elves to make the weekend run smoothly. "Everyone is either family or someone who's worked with us in the past," Jan remarks. Her sister pitches in designing and crafting arrangements, for example, while her brother dresses as an 18th-century caroler and greets guests.

That assignment's no small undertaking—some 4,000 people come to enjoy the crackling fires and the sights and scents of Christmas at Pettengill Farm every year!

"The wait to get into the house can last over 2 hours," Jan reveals. "So we have entertainment in our barn. We also give horse-drawn hayrides in the woods."

Hayrides? How appropriate for an

FLORAL FLAIR is strong suit for Jan Richenburg (top) at holiday time. Thousands flock to annual event at her family's flower farm.

event that sends the senses on a memorable trip to the past *inside* as well.

Editor's Note: *For more information on Jan's Christmas Open House, as well as the farm's schedule of year-round workshops and events, contact Pettengill Farm, 121 Ferry Rd., Salisbury MA 01952; 1-508/462-3675.* ▲

Her Greens Party Spreads Holiday Grins All Around

WHEN it comes to Christmas colors, Gretchen McDaniel of Trumansburg, New York puts the emphasis on the emerald one—with a "greens party" each December.

For 2 days, her family's rural home is transformed into a Santa's workshop. Friends and neighbors take matters into their own hands there…creating holiday wreaths, swags and centerpieces from fresh greenery.

"I don't put everything away until several days later," Gretchen laughs. "People will call afterward wondering if they can make just one more thing!"

In the spirit of the season, Gretchen provides all the supplies. "I get many of them—ribbons, silk flowers, wire, glass balls, candles, baskets—wholesale and pass the savings along," she explains.

"Plus, I use a lot of Douglas fir for wreaths. My mom's sent me Scotch pine from Vermont, too."

The 10-acre spread Gretchen and husband Rich call home also provides some of the merry makings. "I'm able to get large amounts of white pine, blue spruce and boxwood," she notes. "I gather rose hips in the wild and grow perennials as well."

Besides wanting to share her love of Christmas, Gretchen began hosting the party 20 years ago as a money-saver for friends. "I'm just as excited about a centerpiece made from free greens, pinecones and rose hips as I am about an elaborate arrangement," she says.

"Some people make things for friends or decorations for church—there's real variety. One year, a lady made an arrangement to thank someone who'd pulled her car out of a ditch!"

Grown-ups aren't the only ones who have a hand in the event either. The younger McDaniels—Erin, 15, Jason, 13, and Ryan, 10—roll up their sleeves and assist with sorting supplies, babysitting and helping youthful guests.

That's one reason the greens party is so close to Gretchen's heart. "We give of ourselves to those we care about and provide them with something tangible to help celebrate the Christmas season," she observes. "In that way, we're *all* creating memories that will last a lifetime."

Editor's Note: *For details on Gretchen's greens party, contact her at 9342 Rt. 96, Trumansburg NY 14886; 1-607/387-3628.* ▲

DECK THE HALLS! Gretchen McDaniel (second from left above) helps friends and neighbors fashion festive wreaths, greenery garlands and seasonal swags at her yearly holiday greens party.

Simple Gift for Teacher Made Unforgettable Point with Class

By Margaret Taylor of Austin, Texas

AS a teacher in a one-room schoolhouse in 1921, I tutored my pupils in the three R's…until an unusual Christmas present made me realize I needed to add a fourth—*receiving*.

On the day of the class Christmas party that year, the little ones could hardly wait to give me their gifts. They gathered around my desk, clamoring for me to open them.

In due time, I'd torn into each package and found handkerchiefs, pencils and the like. But one boy—Stevie, a frail and shy 6-year-old who'd joined the class just that fall—still sat at his desk tightly clasping a bulky parcel.

"C'mon, Stevie," smirked one of the bigger boys. "Give Miss Stark her present."

Stevie passed me a scared look. Slowly, with eyes downcast, he approached my desk and wordlessly shot out his arm to hand me the box. Then he scurried back to his seat.

Stevie's gift was wrapped in newspaper and tied with a piece of coarse binder twine that had been fashioned into a haphazard bow. "Thank you, Stevie," I said.

The children were all eager to see what the "new kid" had brought. I soon discovered, though, that what the package contained was mainly newspaper, stuffed inside to make the present at a glance seem big. Poor Stevie, I thought.

Finally, after much digging, I unearthed Stevie's gift…a safety pin—a little bent out of shape with a dull point, but still usable. What could I possibly say?

The other students tittered as I walked to Stevie's desk, trying to collect my thoughts. His face was flushed, and I knew that tears of embarrassment were near the surface.

Holding up the pin, I exclaimed, "Look, children! Wasn't this a smart idea? Every lady needs a great big safety pin!"

Relief and pure joy flooded Stevie's face. His eyes were shining, and he smiled proudly at the rest of the class.

With that, the tall boy who had urged Stevie to approach my desk reached across a row of seats toward Stevie and clapped him on the shoulder. "Good thinking, kid," he congratulated.

I knew then that Stevie had helped me teach an important lesson—it doesn't matter how much a present costs but how much feeling is behind it…and even a dull safety pin can have a point worth remembering! ▲

Outgrown Pair of Shoes Spread Joy of Season Across the Miles

By Doris Brecka of Baraboo, Wisconsin

WHEN I was a little girl, we didn't have much to spare—just like most 1930's farm families. But when our teacher told us all the rural school districts would be collecting items to send to needy people in the West, we hurried home excited.

The problem was *what* to send. Our gifts couldn't be perishable foods or home-canned goods that might break during the trip. In our circumstances, that didn't leave much else.

Then we remembered my brother's shoes.

Mom and Dad had bought him a new pair that spring. When summer came, he put them aside so they'd be in good shape for school. A teenage growth spurt, though, left them too tight come fall. Since they were of no use to us girls, they'd make a perfect present!

Mom volunteered to fix a big batch of fudge to send along with them. She packed the candy carefully in a box and slipped the shoes in a brown paper bag.

When Dad suggested putting a note in the bag with our name and address, in the hope we might learn where our gift ended up, we scribbled the information on the box of candy, too.

The next morning, we carried our treasures to school. There, they were added to the offerings of our classmates. Modest as they were, they gave us all a warm feeling.

Weeks passed. With Valentine's Day near, a mysterious letter arrived. Dad, puzzled by the Montana postmark, opened the note addressed to him in painstakingly penciled script.

Inside was a plain piece of tablet paper carrying this message: "The candies were good. The shoes fit fine. It helps the people along a lot."

The signature was a short German surname, much like our own.

What a coincidence! One family had received *both* of our gifts. We, in turn, were touched to think about the sacrifice they'd had to make to buy the stamp for the note.

Of course, with money as tight as it was, we weren't able to send other gifts to that family or even correspond. Still, they were often in our prayers.

Now, some 60 years later, they remain in my mind as a happy memory—the time long ago two families of strangers separated by hundreds of miles shared the true spirit of Christmas. ▲

I REMEMBER WHEN...

Christmas Excitement Was in the Cards

By Helena Stefanski of Lakewood, Colorado

DO YOU recall a time when sending and receiving Christmas cards contained all the excitement of the big day itself? I do!

As a little girl growing up in rural Wyoming, I looked forward each year to the hours we'd spend choosing our holiday cards and composing long letters to accompany them.

Living out in the country, we relied on Christmas catalogs as our "store". With the arrival of each one, Mother and Father eagerly studied the sketches of the cards and closely read the descriptions before placing their order.

When the cards themselves arrived, it felt like Christmas had come early! My brother and I gathered around the table while our parents painstakingly pored over the package. They examined photos in detail and read and re-read each greeting, carefully weighing which card was right for which person.

Back then—in the 1920's—Christmas cards resembled postcards. The front featured brightly colored pictures...Nativity scenes, winter and nature settings, Santa bringing gifts galore in his sleigh or a vintage car, etc. A short verse, printed underneath the picture, was available in many foreign languages. (My family, for instance, sent cards to family and friends in Poland.)

Greetings Grew!

The back of the card, of course, had room for a stamp and the address, plus a small space for personal greetings.

In some cases, though, that tiny area wasn't anywhere near large enough to hold a year's worth of happenings! So we'd tuck the card into an envelope along with a letter.

Handwritten Christmas letters were a treasure in those days. Often, they brought word of family and friends scattered around the world—news that would be shared with others living close by. Marriages, births, plans, reminiscences, even descriptions of daily life made us all feel connected.

Just about the time we began mailing cards, we'd start to receive some, too. Those first few made us eager for more! At our urging, Father picked up the mail more frequently, driving by horse and buggy 2 miles to our post office.

When he returned, we'd clamor around him. Mother read each card out loud, then passed it around for us to admire.

Word of Mouth

Next, she'd gingerly open each letter, since many had delicate Christmas wafers for our Christmas Eve supper enclosed, and update us on the latest family news.

Each and every card was precious. In fact, after the holidays, we'd slip them into special albums. In the years to come, we'd review the cards...and enjoy them all over again!

Yes, I remember Christmas cards of another era. Wouldn't it be nice to bring them—and all they meant—back again?▲

CHRISTMAS GREETINGS

DESIGN COPYRIGHTED...JOHN WINSCH. 1913

WESOŁYCH ŚWIAT

Cuddly Cover Spreads Soothing Seasonal Cheer

WHILE you wait for Santa to make his annual appearance, you can keep comfy and cozy with this attractive afghan and pillow duo.

Marion Kelley of Lansing, Michigan, crocheted the pretty pair that's plenty practical, too. It finishes up in a flash—leaving you plenty of time to stitch a spare set for holiday giving!

Materials Needed (for afghan):
Worsted-weight yarn in 3-1/2-ounce skeins—10 skeins each of red and green*
Size P (10mm) crochet hook
Yarn needle

Materials Needed (for pillow):
Worsted-weight yarn in 3-1/2-ounce skeins—2 skeins each of red and green
Size P (10mm) crochet hook
Yarn needle
12-inch x 16-inch pillow form

*Marion used Coats and Clark Classic

Yarn in No. 902 Jockey Red and No. 686 Paddy Green.

Finished Size: Afghan is about 49 inches wide x 71 inches long. Pillow is about 17-1/2 inches wide x 12 inches long.

Gauge: Working with two strands together, 7 dc sts = 4 inches.

Directions:
AFGHAN: With two strands of red held together, ch 121.

Row 1: Dc in third ch from hook (counts as dc), dc in each ch across: 119 sts.

Rows 2-4: With red, ch 3 (counts as dc here and throughout), turn; working in back loops only, dc in each dc across: 119 sts.

Row 5: Add two strands of green to the two strands of red to make a total of four strands; ch 1, turn; working in both loops with all four strands, (sc in next st, ch 1, skip next st) across to last st, sc in last st.

Row 6: Ch 1, turn, sc in next st, (sc in next ch-1 sp, ch 1, skip next st) across to last 2 sts, sc in last ch-1 sp, sc in last st.

Row 7: Fasten off both strands of red; with green, ch 2, turn, dc in each sc and ch-1 sp across: 119 sts.

Rows 8-10: Ch 2, turn, working in back loops only, dc in each dc across.

Rows 11-12: Repeat Rows 5-6, adding two strands of red in Row 11.

Row 13: Fasten off both strands of green; with red, ch 2, turn, dc in each sc and ch-1 sp across: 119 sts.

Rows 14-46: Repeat Rows 2-13 two more times, then rows 2-10 once. Do not fasten off.

EDGING:

Round 1: Repeat Row 11 without turning at end of row; ch 1, sc in corner, ch 1, (sc in end of next row, ch 1) 38 times evenly spaced along end to next corner, (sc, ch 1) in corner st; turn corner and continue working Row 11 on opposite side of Row 1, ch 1, sc in corner st, ch 1, (sc in end of next row, ch 1) 38 times evenly spaced along opposite side to beginning corner, ch 1, slip st in top of beginning sc.

Round 2: Ch 1, turn, (sc in next ch-1 sp, ch 1) around afghan, working (sc, ch 1, sc, ch 1) in each corner st, slip st to top of beginning sc. Fasten off and weave in all yarn ends.

PILLOW: With two strands of red held together, ch 51.

Row 1: Dc in third ch from hook (counts as dc here and throughout), dc in each ch across: 49 sts.

Rows 2-13: Repeat Afghan Rows 2-13: 49 sts.

Rows 14-16: Repeat Rows 2-4. Do not fasten off.

Pillow Finishing: Seam Row 1: Add two strands of green to the two strands of red, ch 1, turn, fold pillow piece in half and working through both layers together, (sc in next st, ch 1, skip next st) across to last st, sc in last st.

Seam Row 2: Repeat Afghan Row 6. Fasten off.

Attach two strands of each color to the opposite end of the pillow and repeat Seam Rows 1 and 2. Weave in all yarn ends.

Insert pillow form and sew remaining seam, using matching yarn. ▲

ABBREVIATIONS:	
ch	chain
dc	double crochet
sc	single crochet
sp	space
st(s)	stitch(es)

Christmas Cozy Keeps Its Cool When Heat's On

THERE'S no need to get out of the kitchen if you can't stand the heat! Reach for a seasonally shaded knitted cozy to keep your teapot warm…and your fingers cool.

Louise Purpura of Valparaiso, Indiana—a devoted knitter *and* tea drinker who creates cozies for every season of the year—stitched this special one in the sprightly colors of Christmas. It's sure to delight the tea lover on your list.

Materials Needed:
Worsted-weight yarn—one skein of
*   dark green (A) and 1 ounce*
*   each of red (B) and white (C)*
Pair of size 8 (5mm) knitting needles
*   or size needed to obtain correct*
*   gauge*
Size C/2 (2.75/3mm) crochet hook
Tapestry needle
Scissors
Teapot

Finished Size: Tea cozy will fit a 6-1/2-inch to 7-inch teapot.

Gauge: When working in St st, 4 sts = 1 inch and 11 rows = 2 inches.

KNITTING REMINDERS:
Changing colors: Carry yarn not in use loosely across wrong side of work.
Stockinette stitch: St st
    Row 1 (RS): Knit
    Row 2 (WS): Purl
    Repeat Rows 1 and 2.
K 2, p 2 ribbing:
    Every Row: (K 2, p 2) across row.

Directions:
With straight knitting needles and A, cast on 80 sts.
    Rows 1-6: Work in k 2, p 2 ribbing.
    Rows 7-8: With B, work in St st.
    Rows 9-10: With A, work in St st.
    Rows 11-12: With B, work in St st.
    Rows 13-16: With A, work in St st.
    Row 17: (K 5 with A, k 1 with C) across row.
    Rows 18-20: With A, work in St st, beginning with a WS row.
    Row 21: K 2 with A, (k 1 with C, k 5 with A) across row.
    Rows 22-24: With A, work in St st, beginning with a WS row.
    Rows 25-32: Repeat Rows 17-24.
    Rows 33-38: Repeat Rows 7-12.
    Row 39: With A, work in St st.
    Dec Row 40: (P 2 tog) across row: 30 sts.
    Dec Row 41: (K 2 tog) across row: 15 sts.
    Dec Row 42: (P 2 tog) to last st, p 1: 8 sts.
    Dec Row 43: (K 2 tog) across row: 4 sts.
    Dec Row 44: (P 2 tog) twice: 2 sts.
    Dec Row 45: K last 2 sts tog.
    Cut yarn, leaving a 20-in. end. Thread tapestry needle with yarn end and draw through remaining 7 sts; fasten securely on wrong side. Stitch seam of hat from top to bottom edge, using matching yarn ends for each row and leaving a 2-in. hole unstitched 2-1/2 in. from the bottom edge of the cozy for the teapot spout. (Check your teapot for correct positioning of the spout hole.)
    Weave in remaining yarn ends.
    Hanging Loop: With B, chain 27. Fasten off, leaving an 8-in. yarn end. Fold chain in half and use yarn end to stitch both ends of chain to top center of tea cozy. ▲

ABBREVIATIONS:	
dec	decrease
k	knit
p	purl
RS	right side
st(s)	stitch(es)
St st	Stockinette stitch
tog	together
WS	wrong side

Craft Section...

Directions:

Pre-wash and machine-dry all fabrics.

CUTTING: Enlarge the pattern on this page by tracing onto tracing or pattern paper marked with 1-in. squares or use a copy machine capable of enlarging to 200% (each square will be 1 in.). Cut fabrics as directed with pattern.

Also cut two 12-1/2-in. squares each from Christmas print and solid-color fabrics.

ASSEMBLY: Pieces include 1/4-in. seam allowances. Sew seams with a small straight stitch, placing right sides together and backstitching at the beginning and end of each seam.

Pin, then baste lace along curved edge on right side of Christmas print flap piece, having right sides together and raw edge of flap matching gathered edge of lace. Pin Christmas print flap piece to solid-color lining flap piece, matching edges with lace between layers. Stitch along curved edge. Turn right side out and press.

Making two small pleats in the lace at each corner for extra fullness, baste the remaining pre-gathered lace to all edges of one Christmas print (backing) square, having right sides together and raw edge of flap matching gathered edge of lace. Overlap ends, trimming off any excess lace.

Pin straight raw edges of the flap pieces to one edge of the backing square with right sides of fabric together and lace between layers.

Add a solid-color (lining) square to the backing piece, right sides together. Pin along flap edge with flap between layers. Pin the second solid-color square along one edge to the right side of the remaining Christmas print (front) square. Stitch along pinned edge of each. Fold lining to wrong side of pieces, matching raw edges. Press.

Keeping flap out of the way, pin backing to front square, Christmas print sides together. Stitch side and bottom edges together. Trim corners. Finish seam with zigzagging or overcasting. Turn right side out and press.

With flap up, hand-stitch each upper corner together, stitching top front edge to top back lining edge for 1/2 in. so front won't "peek" out at the corners.

Sew button onto the lower edge of the flap, referring to photo above for placement. Hand-sew the piece of hook Velcro to the lining side of the flap underneath the button. To finish the closure, hand-sew the piece of loop Velcro to the front piece only under the hook Velcro.

Open flap and insert pillow or pillow form. Then give your sofa or favorite chair a lively holiday look! ▲

Colorful Christmasy Cover Buttons Up Plush Pillows

SLIP into the Christmas spirit…with this stylish slipcover. It stitches up in a flash to spiff up your sofa or stuff in a stocking!

Winnie Malone of Westerville, Ohio shares the directions for the clever endeavor, one that stretches your decorating dollar and won't tax your storage space.

Materials Needed:

Pattern on this page
Tracing or pattern paper
Pencil
Ruler
1/2 yard each of Christmas print fabric and coordinating solid-color fabric (for lining)
2 yards of 1-1/2-inch-wide pre-gathered lace (to match your fabric)
1-inch to 1-1/2-inch button (color of choice)
Velcro dot or 1/2 inch of 5/8-inch Velcro
Matching thread
Standard sewing supplies
12-inch pillow or pillow form

Finished Size: Pillow cover is 12 inches square.

FLAP PATTERN

Cut 1 on fold after enlarging pattern—Christmas print

Cut 1 on fold after enlarging pattern—solid color fabric (lining)

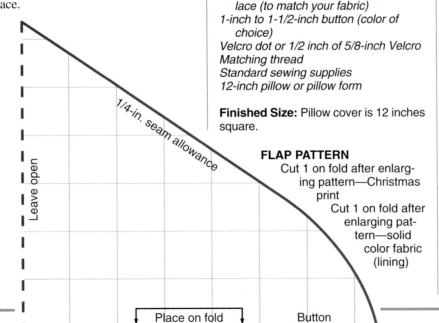

1/4-in. seam allowance

Leave open

Place on fold

Button

Scrappy Soldier Lights Up Yule Decor

ENLIST a little aid from this bright idea and you'll drum up a full complement of holiday cheer!

"I love to find ways to use things in my crafts that I already have around the house," says Ginger Bush of Franklin, North Carolina. "This soldier—made from a used light bulb and a bathroom tissue tube—is inexpensive to put together…and a great way to recycle."

Ginger's project is such fast fun, you may want to assemble a whole regiment. No matter what your Yuletide decor, they'll "fall in" colorfully.

Materials Needed:
Patterns on this page
Pencil
Tracing paper
Ruler
Bathroom tissue tube, 4-1/2 inches long x 1-1/2 inches in diameter
One used light bulb
Felt pieces—black, dark red, red and pink
Scraps of black fake fur
1/8-inch black satin ribbon, 6-1/4 inches long
Black thread
Scraps of various gold braids or rickrack (whatever you have on hand for embellishing soldier's coat)
Three toothpicks
Two 3/8-inch beads or red pom-poms
Acrylic craft paints—flesh, black, dark red and red
Paintbrushes—fine liner and medium

Spray acrylic varnish or sealer
Scissors
Tacky (white) glue
Sewing machine (optional)

Directions:
CUTTING: Trace patterns onto tracing paper and cut out pieces for soldier's hat, hands and feet as directed on patterns. From black felt, cut a 6-1/4-in. x 2-1/4-in. pants piece. From red felt, cut two 1-1/2-in. x 2-3/4-in. arm pieces and a 3-in. x 6-3/4-in. jacket piece. Round lower corners of jacket piece.

PAINTING: Paint glass of light bulb with flesh paint. When dry, add face as follows, referring to photo at left for placement: Dot on black eyes with handle end of brush. Use fine liner to add red mouth and black nose. Let dry. Use a toothpick to add white dots to top right of each eye. Paint dark red cheeks. Let dry. Spray all sides of bulb with varnish or sealer and let dry.

ASSEMBLY: Run a bead of glue around rim of one end of bathroom tissue tube. Insert light bulb into the tube to make head and body. Let dry.

Glue pants piece around the bottom edge of the tube, overlapping short ends in back. Run a bead of glue around the bottom edge of the tube and set tube onto center of feet piece. Let dry.

Glue coat piece around the top of the tube so the short ends overlap in front and straight long edge is even with top edge of tube.

Glue the piece of black ribbon around the waist 1-3/4 in. from upper edge for the soldier's belt. Then glue a small piece of gold trim in the center of the belt to make the buckle.

To make each arm, roll one arm piece lengthwise into a tube. Glue long edges together. Repeat for second arm.

Glue one finished arm onto each side of the soldier, making sure the seams are against the soldier's coat.

Fold a hand piece in half. Run a bead of glue along the short ends and insert them into the end of the arm. Repeat with the second hand piece into the end of the opposite arm.

Embellish the jacket using gold braid or rickrack (refer to photo or use your own design).

Make drumsticks by gluing a bead or pom-pom to the end of each toothpick (painting bead red and allowing to dry if needed). Then glue the opposite end of a drumstick between the folds of each of the soldier's hands. (You may also sub-

stitute a miniature drum, horn, etc. for the drumsticks.)

Referring to photo for placement, glue a piece of gold braid curving under the soldier's chin and around the sides of the face.

With right sides together, use a 1/8-in. seam to sew the hat pieces together, machine-sewing or hand-sewing with a running stitch (Fig. 1) and leaving bottom edge open as shown on pattern. Turn the hat right side out, then glue it to the soldier's head so it meets the ends of the gold braid. ▲

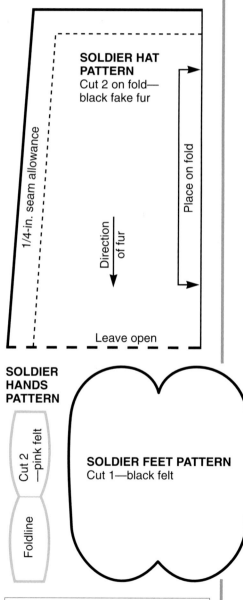

SOLDIER HAT PATTERN
Cut 2 on fold—black fake fur

1/4-in. seam allowance

Direction of fur

Place on fold

Leave open

SOLDIER HANDS PATTERN

Cut 2—pink felt

Foldline

SOLDIER FEET PATTERN
Cut 1—black felt

Fig. 1
Running stitch

Claus Keeps the Mess Off Tiny Tyke's Holiday Best

SINCE everyone else dresses up for Christmas dinner, why can't baby, too? That's what Bertha Harris of Southern Pines, North Carolina asked herself before designing this machine-washable bib. Pretty, practical and bursting with holiday cheer, it'll delight any tiny tot—and mom—on your gift list.

Materials Needed:

Pattern on next page
Tracing or pattern paper
Pencil
Invisible tape
1/2 yard of white flannel
7-inch x 10-inch piece of red pin dot fabric
4-inch x 7-inch piece of pink solid fabric
Paper-backed fusible web
Tear-away stabilizer or typing paper
Velcro dot or 1/2 inch of 5/8-inch Velcro
Black and red embroidery floss
Embroidery needle
Matching thread
Standard sewing supplies

Directions:

Pre-wash and machine-dry all fabrics.

CUTTING: Enlarge the pattern on the next page by tracing on pattern paper or tracing paper marked with 1-in. squares or use a copy machine capable of enlarging to 200% (each square will be 1 in.). Fold pattern or tracing paper and copy pattern to complete as in Fig. 1. Cut three bib pieces out of flannel with this completed pattern.

APPLIQUEING: Trace face, hat and nose applique patterns onto paper side of fusible web, adding under-lap to face piece as indicated by dotted line on pattern. Cut out all shapes, leaving a 1/2-in. margin around each piece. Place fusible web shapes on wrong side of each appropriate fabric (as indicated on pattern) and fuse in place, following manufacturer's instructions. Cut out pieces and peel off paper backing. Referring to pattern for placement, position pieces on one flannel bib piece. Fuse in place. Position tear-away stabilizer on wrong side behind applique pieces.

Use matching thread and medium satin zigzag setting on machine to applique in this order: face, nose and straight edges of red pin dot "hat" pieces. Pull all thread ends to back of work and secure. Remove stabilizer or typing paper.

EMBROIDERY: Separate six-strand floss and use three strands for all embroidery. Referring to pattern for placement, use stem stitch (Fig. 2) to hand-embroider black eyes and red mouth.

ASSEMBLY: Place remaining two flannel pieces on top of the appliqued piece, right sides together. Stitch around all edges with a 1/4-in. seam, stitching through all three layers and leaving an opening at the bottom as indicated on pattern. Clip curves. Turn right side out. Fold the opening edges in 1/4 in. and hand-stitch the opening closed. Press.

Hand-stitch the loop side of the Velcro piece to the end of the right side of the left-hand curve of the hat as shown in Fig. 1. Hand-stitch the hook side of the Velcro piece to the wrong side of the right-hand curve of the hat to finish the closure.

Quilt by straight-stitching through all layers along dashed lines on pattern. ▲

APPLIQUE KEY
— Outline of piece
– – Pieces under overlap of other piece
— Embroidery details
- - - Quilting lines

Fig. 1
Completing bib pattern

Hat   Hat

Face

Nose

Fig. 2
Stem stitch

SANTA BIB/APPLIQUE PATTERN
BIB: Cut 3 after completing pattern (Fig. 1)—white flannel
FACE/NOSE: Trace 1 of each after completing pattern—paper-backed fusible web
HAT: Trace 2 (1 for each side)—paper-backed fusible web

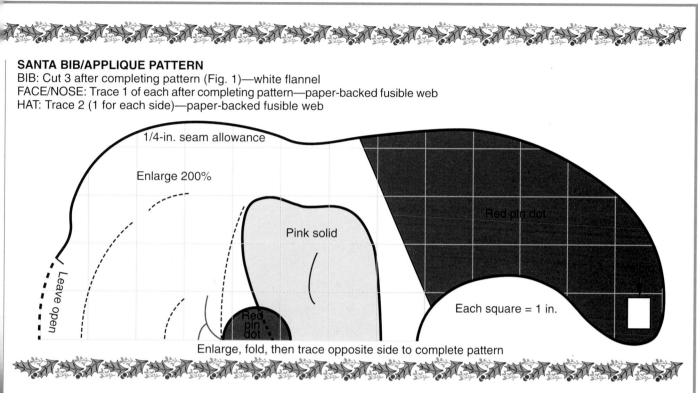

1/4-in. seam allowance

Enlarge 200%

Pink solid

Red pin dot

Leave open

Red pin dot

Velcro

Each square = 1 in.

Enlarge, fold, then trace opposite side to complete pattern

Yo-Yo Tree Adds Fun to Festivities

PUT a new spin on your holiday decorating with a traditional crafting favorite—yo-yos! LuElla Reimer of Hillsboro, Kansas cultivated the idea for this Christmas tree wall hanging using pin dot fabric and a spirited border print.

Materials Needed:
*44-inch-wide or scraps of 100% cotton
  or cotton/polyester fabrics—
  1/2 yard of unbleached muslin,
  3/4 yard of green pin dot fabric,
  scrap of brown pin dot fabric and
  3-1/2-inch x 18-inch piece of
  Christmas border or print of choice
20-inch square of bonded batting
Pom-poms—one 1/2-inch white and
  ten 1/2-inch red
5/8-inch white plastic ring for hanging
Matching thread
Standard sewing supplies
Tacky (white) glue*

Finished Size: Wall hanging is about 16 inches wide x 17 inches high.

Directions:
Pre-wash and machine-dry all fabrics.
  CUTTING: From both green pin dot fabric (back) and muslin (front), cut a 16-1/2-in. x 19-in. triangle (see Fig. 1).
  Cut ten 4-5/8-in. circles from the green pin dot fabric. Cut one 4-5/8-in. circle from the brown pin dot fabric.
  YO-YOS: Fold the edge of each yo-yo fabric circle under 3/16 in. with your thumb as you use a short running stitch

(Fig. 2) to stitch around the circle, leaving long thread ends. Pull thread ends tightly to gather center to a 1/2-in. opening, then tie thread ends together to secure and clip ends close to knot. Flatten yo-yo with your fingers with opening centered as shown in Fig. 3.
  ASSEMBLY: Press under 1/4 in. along top edge of Christmas border or print. Pin border or print to lower edge of muslin front triangle, matching long raw edge and allowing border or print ends to extend evenly on both ends. Edge-stitch top folded edge to muslin front triangle. Trim ends of border or print even with edges of muslin front triangle.
  Referring to the photo at right, pin the green pin dot yo-yos in rows forming a tree shape on the muslin front triangle, adding the brown pin dot yo-yo as a tree trunk. Hand-tack yo-yos in place where edges of each touch adjoining yo-yos.
  With right sides together, place the front and back triangles right sides together on top of the piece of batting. Sew all sides of the triangles together, leaving a 4-in. opening on the bottom for turning. Turn the triangles right side out and hand-stitch the opening closed.
  Place a dot of glue in the center of the green pin dot yo-yos and add a red pom-pom to each one. Glue the white pom-pom in the center of the brown pin dot yo-yo with a dot of glue.
  For hanging, stitch the plastic ring to the green pin dot back of the triangle just below the point. ▲

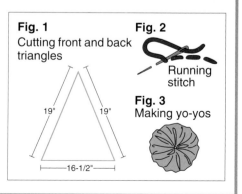

Fig. 1
Cutting front and back triangles

19"   19"

16-1/2"

Fig. 2

Running stitch

Fig. 3
Making yo-yos

Dynamic Duo Chases Winter's Chill with Cheer

YOUNG ONES will keep Old Man Winter at bay in festive fashion when you crochet this cozy cap and scarf set for them.

Karen Taylor of Redding, California designed the perky pair to suit any child on your gift list.

Materials Needed:
Worsted-weight acrylic yarn in 3-1/2-ounce skeins—three skeins of green and one each of red and white*
Size F/5 (3.75mm) crochet hook
Size H/8 (5mm) crochet hook (optional)
Tapestry needle
Scissors

*Karen used Red Heart Classic Yarn in No. 1 White, No. 686 Paddy Green and No. 912 Cherry Red.

Gauge: With size F hook in sc, 7 sts and 8 rows = 2 inches.

Special Stitches: SINGLE CROCHET 2 STITCHES TOGETHER (sc 2 sts tog): Insert hook in next st, draw up a loop, repeat in next st (3 loops on hook), yo and draw through all 3 loops on hook to complete.
TRIPLE CROCHET 2 STITCHES TOGETHER (tr 2 sts tog): * Yo twice and insert hook in next st, draw up a loop, (yo, draw through 2 loops) twice *, repeat between *'s in next st (3 loops on hook), yo, draw through all loops on hook.
TRIPLE CROCHET 3 STITCHES TOGETHER (tr 3 sts tog): Work as for tr 2 sts tog, repeating between *'s in next *2 sts* (4 loops on hook), yo, draw through all loops on hook.
CHANGING COLORS: For hat, join new colors with sl st in beginning st of previous round. For scarf, join new colors with sl st in last st of previous row.

Directions:
HAT: With green and F hook, ch 11.
Ribbing Row 1: Sc in 2nd ch from hook and in each ch across.
Ribbing Row 2: Working in back loops only, ch 1, turn, sc in each sc across.
Repeat Ribbing Row 2 until piece measures 16-1/2 in. long. Bring short ends together. Join with a sl st in front loop of row closest to you and back loop

of back row, stitching first and last rows together. Continue across edge.
Round 1: Working in ends of ribbing rows, work 60 sc evenly spaced around ribbing, join with sl st in top of beginning sc.
Rounds 2-10: Ch 1, turn, sc in each sc across, join with sl st in top of beginning sc.
Round 11: Ch 1, turn, sc in first st, * dc in next st, 3 tr in next st, dc in next st, sc in next st, repeat from * around, omitting last sc, join with sl st in top of beginning sc. Fasten off.
Round 12: Join white, ch 3, work tr in base of ch-3 until 2 loops remain on hook, tr in next st until 3 loops remain on hook, yo, pull through all loops, * dc in next st, sc in next st, dc in next st, tr next 3 sts tog, repeat from * around, omitting last tr next 3 sts tog, join with sl st in top of beginning tr. Fasten off.
Round 13: Join red, ch 1, sc in each st around, join with sl st in top of beginning sc: 60 sc. Fasten off.
Round 14: Join white, ch 1, sc in each st around, join with sl st in top of beginning sc.
Rounds 15-18: Ch 1, turn, sc in each st around, join with sl st in top of beginning sc. Fasten off.
Round 19: Join red, ch 1, sc in each st around, join with sl st in top of beginning sc. Fasten off.
Round 20: Join white, ch 1, turn, (sc in next 2 sts, sc next 2 sts tog) around, join with sl st in top of beginning sc: 45 sts.
Round 21: Repeat Round 11.
Round 22: Join green, ch 3, tr in next st, * dc in next st, sc in next st, dc in next st, tr next 3 sts tog, repeat from * to last 5 sts, dc in next st, sc in next st, dc in next st, work tr in next dc until 2 loops remain on hook, join with sl st in top of beginning tr.
Round 23: Ch 1, turn, (sc in next 2 sts, sc next 2 sts tog) around, join with sl st in top of beginning sc: 33 sts.
Round 24: Ch 1, turn, (sc in next 2 sts, sc next 2 sts tog) to last st, sc in last st, join with sl st in top of beginning sc: 25 sts.
Round 25: Ch 1, turn, (sc in next st, sc next 2 sts tog) to last st, sc in last st, join with sl st in top of beginning sc: 17 sts.
Round 26: Ch 1, turn, (sc in next st, sc next 2 sts tog) to last 2 sts, sc last 2

sts tog, join with sl st in top of beginning sc: 11 sc.
Round 27: Ch 1, turn, (sc 2 sts tog) around to last st, sc in last st: 6 sts. Fasten off, leaving a long yarn end.
Finishing: Use yarn end to gather up remaining sts. Use matching yarn ends to sew back seam. Weave in remaining yarn ends.
Cross-Stitching: Follow chart by working cross-stitches around white band of Rows 14-18, making each cross-stitch so it covers a single sc st as in Fig. 1 on next page, beginning one stitch to left of back seam and repeating chart around band. Each sc st counts as one square on chart and is stitched with a single strand of red yarn and tapestry needle.

Do not knot yarn on back of work. Instead, leave a short tail on back of work and hold in place. Weave tails and ends through several stitches as stitching progresses.
Tassel: For tassel, cut ten 12-in. pieces each of red and white yarns. Tie them together in center with another 12-in. piece of yarn, holding ends of this piece out. Fold yarn pieces in half and tie again 1 in. down from center tie to form head of tassel. Trim ends to about 5 in. long. Using ends of yarn center tie, attach tassel to top center of hat.
SCARF: With green, ch 26.
Row 1: Sc in 2nd ch from hook and in each ch across: 25 sts.
Rows 2-18: Ch 1, turn, sc in each sc across.
Row 19: Ch 1, turn, sc in first st, * dc in next st, 3 tr in next st, dc in next st, sc in next st, repeat from * across. Fasten off.
Row 20: Join white, ch 4 (counts as tr here and throughout), turn, tr in next st, * dc in next st, sc in next st, dc in next st, tr next 3 sts tog, repeat from * to last 2 sts, omitting last (tr next 3 sts tog), tr last 2 sts tog. Fasten off.

Row 21: Join red, ch 1, turn, sc in each st across: 25 sc. Fasten off.

Rows 22-26: Join white, ch 1, turn, sc in each st across. Fasten off at end of Row 26.

Row 27: Join red, ch 1, turn, sc in each sc across. Fasten off.

Row 28: Join white, ch 4, turn, tr in base of ch-4, * dc in next st, sc in next st, dc in next st, 3 tr in next st, repeat from * across, ending with 2 tr in last st: 37 sts. Fasten off.

Row 29: Join green, ch 1, turn, sc in first st, * dc in next st, tr 3 tog in next st, dc in next st, sc in next st, repeat from * across: 25 sts.

Rows 30-145: Ch 1, turn, sc in each st across (116 rows).

Rows 146-156: Repeat Rows 19-29.

Rows 157-174: Ch 1, turn, sc in each sc across.

Finishing: With tapestry needle, weave in yarn ends.

Cross-Stitching: Repeat as directed for hat, making red cross-stitches across white bands of Rows 22-26 at ends of scarf, beginning one stitch in from edge and repeating chart across bands.

Fringe: Cut 52 strands each of white and red yarn, making each one 12 in. long. Hold two white and two red yarn strands together and fold in half. Using H hook, pull folds from back to front through one corner stitch. Insert yarn ends through loop formed and pull to tighten. Repeat between *every other stitch* across both ends of scarf. Trim ends. ▲

COZY CAP AND SCARF
COLOR KEY	Coats & Clark
☐ White	1
■ Cherry Red	912

COZY CAP AND SCARF CHART

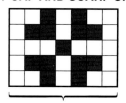

Repeat across or around

Fig. 1 Cross-stitch on single crochet

Rag Wreath's Hearty Welcome

IF your heart's set on a nice new country Christmas accent, but your budget's not, don't despair. Just fetch a few festive fabric scraps and start in on this project that's both pretty and penny-pinching.

Brenda Richman of Alexandria, Minnesota won the hearts of shoppers at her hometown holiday craft sale with her crafty recycling method.

Materials Needed:
Wire hanger
Wire cutter
3 yards of 3/4-inch cotton cording
1/8 yard of 44-inch-wide cotton Christmas fabrics—three or more different designs (Brenda used seven different fabrics)
2-1/2-inch x 24-inch piece of coordinating fabric torn for bow
Rag rug or any large-eyed needle
Masking tape
Glue gun
Scissors

Finished Size: Wreath is about 11 inches wide x 12 inches high.

Directions:
Cut wire hanger to remove hanger loop.

Beginning at center top, bend remaining wire into a 10-1/2 -in. x 10-1/2-in. heart shape. Tape ends together.

Rip the 1/8-yd. fabric pieces into 3/4-in.-wide x 44-in.-long strips by first folding the fabric in half, both selvages together. Then clip the fold at 3/4-in. intervals and rip fabric toward the selvages.

Starting at the top center of the heart, tape beginning of cotton cording to wire for 1 in. Wrap fabric strips around cording and heart-shaped wire, overlapping just enough to hide cotton cording.

When the end of a fabric strip is reached, choose a strip of a different fabric and continue wrapping, wrapping over 2 in. of the end of the used strip and 2 in. of the beginning of the new strip.

After you've wrapped the cording around the wire heart, continue wrapping the cording separately above the heart, wrapping for 2 to 3 in.

Now make a t-knot with the same strip, as follows: Wrap strip around both rows of cording, then bring the needle down between the rows of cording to the right of first stitch of knot. Come up to left of first stitch and go back down to the right of that stitch. The knot should now look like a "t". Continue wrapping, making t-knots every 2 to 3 in.

When you reach the bottom of the heart, make a point, curving back up and bringing cord over top of the first row of the heart, bringing it to inside of that row. Continue wrapping as before.

When you reach the top of the heart, you will end up below the first row. Cut the cording so it lines up with the first row on the opposite side. Wrap entire cording and make a t-knot in the point of the heart. Tuck ends under and glue them down. Let dry.

Tie a bow with the 2-1/2-in. x 24-in. piece of fabric. Glue bow to top of heart covering t-knot made in the point. Let dry.

Angel's Appropriate Accent For Season Filled with Spirit

USHERING IN a celestial celebration is easy. Just stitch up this adorable angel that's oh-sew-sweet!

Designer Brenda Richman of Alexandria, Minnesota helped the cheerful cherub get her wings. "Add an angelic touch to your Christmas by hanging her on a wall or nestling her on a shelf or mantel," Brenda advises.

Then, for one that lasts all year-round, stitch up a spare in colors to match your everyday decor.

Materials Needed:
Patterns on these two pages
Tracing or pattern paper
Ruler
Pencil
44-inch-wide 100% cotton fabrics—
  1/2 yard of Christmas print of your choice (for dress) and 1/2 yard of bleached muslin
2 yards of 1/8-inch-wide gold ribbon (or 1 yard each of two different gold ribbons)
4 inches of 1/8-inch-wide ribbon (for hanger)
Wavy wool (for hair)
24 inches of mini-star garland
11-inch x 8-inch piece of batting
Polyester stuffing
Glue gun and glue sticks
Fine-line permanent black marker
Matching thread
Standard sewing supplies

Finished Size: Angel is about 18 inches tall.

Directions:
Pre-wash and machine-dry all fabrics.

CUTTING: Trace patterns onto tracing or pattern paper, then cut out patterns. Cut out fabrics as directed on pattern pieces.

In addition to the patterns, cut two 30-in. x 5-in. pieces of muslin for the dress fringe. Cut one 14-in. x 30-in. piece of print fabric for the dress. Cut two 10-in. x 6-in. pieces of print fabric for the sleeves.

ASSEMBLY: Use 1/4-in. seams throughout. Sew seams with a small straight stitch, placing right sides together and backstitching at the beginning and end of each seam.

Body/Arms: Sew the two body pieces together, leaving bottom open for turning. Clip to neck. Turn body right side out and firmly stuff to 1 in. from opening edges. Bring opening edges together and stitch 1/4 in. from raw edges.

Sew the arm pieces together in pairs, leaving the tops open for turning. Clip below thumb. Turn the arms right side out and lightly stuff until 4 in. of arms are stuffed. Bring opening edges together and stitch 1/4 in. from raw edges.

Wings: Place the two wing pieces right sides together on top of the 11-in. x 8-in. piece of batting. Sew the wings together, leaving a 2-in. opening at center for turning. Clip to seam. Turn the wings right side out so the batting layer is inside between the two layers of fabric. Fold opening edges in 1/4 in. and hand-

stitch the opening closed. Topstitch lines on wings as shown on pattern.

Fringe: Fold both 30-in. x 5-in. muslin pieces in half lengthwise and press. Fringe by making 2-in. cuts every 1/4 in. along both 30-in. lengths of fabric. Wet pieces and dry them in the dryer to curl the ends.

Dress: Pin one strip of fringe so fold is 1/2 in. above lower edge of 30-in. x 14-in. print dress piece. Stitch 1/4 in. from fold through fringe and dress layers. In the same manner, add the second strip of fringe 1/2 in. above the first strip.

Fold the dress piece in half, right sides together, then sew the short edges

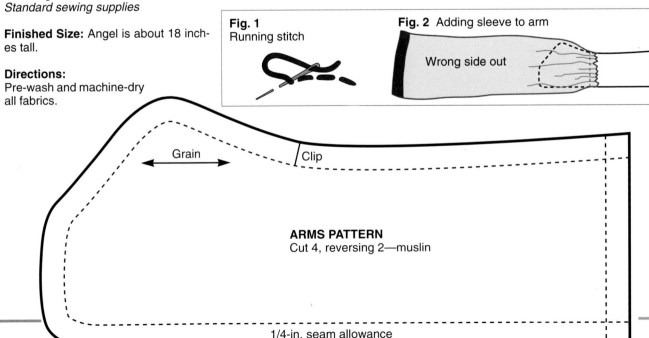

Fig. 1
Running stitch

Fig. 2 Adding sleeve to arm

Wrong side out

Grain

Clip

ARMS PATTERN
Cut 4, reversing 2—muslin

1/4-in. seam allowance

of the piece together, forming a tube. Turn the dress right side out and make a running stitch 1/8 in. from the top edge (see Fig. 1), leaving long thread ends for gathering. Place the dress around the body and gather to fit the angel's neck. Fasten off ends and cut them short. Glue the upper edge of the dress to the neck. Let dry.

Sleeves: With right sides together, sew the short edges of each 10-in. x 6-in. print sleeve piece together, forming tubes. With the tubes still inside out, make a running stitch 1/8 in. from one (bottom) edge of each sleeve, leaving long thread ends for gathering.

Place one tube around an arm as in Fig. 2 and gather up to fit the wrist. Glue in place. Let dry, then turn the tube right side out. Repeat this process with the other sleeve and arm.

Attach an arm to the angel by bring- ing the raw edges of the sleeve togeth- er (with arm inside) and gluing them to the dress at the neck, making sure the thumb is pointing forward. Let dry. At- tach the other arm in the same manner.

FINISHING: Cut the 2-yd. piece of 1/8-in. gold ribbon in half to make two 1-yd. pieces (or use the 1-yd. pieces). Holding both pieces of ribbon together, wrap them around the angel's neck and tie them in a bow at center front. Se- cure bow with a small bead of glue at the neck.

Glue desired amount of wavy wool to head for hair. Let dry. Bend the star garland into a 2-3/4-in. circle to form the halo and glue it to the angel's head with a small amount of glue. Let dry.

Form a loop with the 4-in. length of 1/8-in. ribbon and glue it to the upper back of the angel's dress to make the hanger. Let dry.

Glue the wings on the back of the an- gel so the top center is touching the neckline and covering the bottom of the hanger. Let dry.

Referring to photo and pattern, draw the angel's face with the black marker. ▲

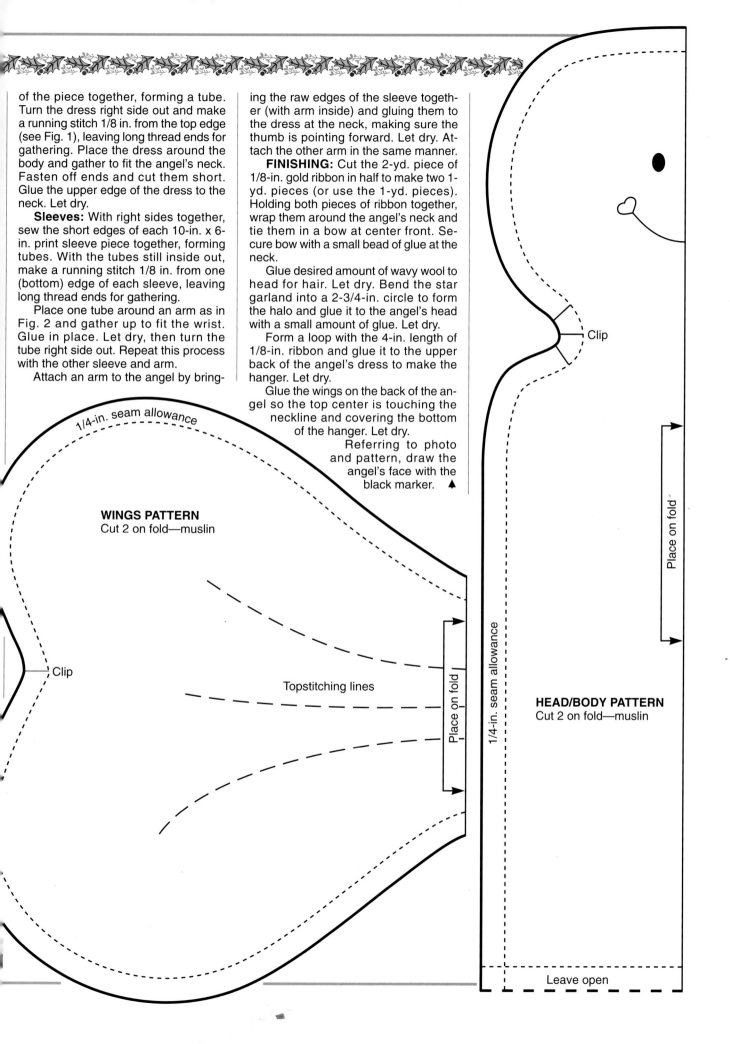

Clip

1/4-in. seam allowance

WINGS PATTERN
Cut 2 on fold—muslin

Clip

Topstitching lines

Place on fold

Place on fold

1/4-in. seam allowance

Place on fold

HEAD/BODY PATTERN
Cut 2 on fold—muslin

Leave open

Nativity Gives A New Twist To Christmas

THE REAL REASON for the season will receive the attention it's due when you craft this creative creche, assures Loretta Kemna of St. Elizabeth, Missouri. She reverently rendered the manger scene from pretty paper twist, and it's become a Yuletide favorite with her family.

Materials Needed:

3-1/2-inch-wide to 4-inch-wide paper twist—1-1/4 yards of ivory, 1 yard each of light blue and medium blue and 1/2 yard of red
Wooden beads—two 1-inch and one 1/2-inch
Chenille stem or pipe cleaner (any color), cut into two 5-inch lengths
12-inch length of twine
Seven jumbo craft sticks, each 3/4 inch x 6 inches
Dark brown and dark auburn curly crepe doll hair
Small amount of excelsior
6-inch twig
Scissors
Glue gun and glue sticks or thick tacky (white) glue
Ruler
Ivory and blue thread

Directions:

BASE: Lay five craft sticks side by side. To fasten them together, cut the other two craft sticks to 3-1/2-in. lengths and lay on both ends of the base about 1 in. from the ends of the five parallel sticks. Glue in place. When dry, turn over so 3-1/2-in. pieces are on bottom of base.

FIGURES: Cut each piece of paper twist the full width of the twist unless otherwise indicated.

Joseph: Cut one 12-in. and one 6-in. piece of ivory, one 5-1/2-in. and two 12-in. pieces of medium blue and one 12-in. piece of red.

Untwist all strips and use right or darker side out (if there is a right side). Use matching thread to tie pieces.

Place a 1-in. wooden bead in the center of the 12-in. ivory piece. Fold paper crosswise over bead, matching cut ends. Pull down and twist piece so it fits tightly to bead, smoothing out a face side. To form head and body, wrap thread around twist just below bead. Knot thread ends together and cut thread ends close.

Place a 5-in. chenille stem or pipe cleaner piece over one side edge of the 6-in. ivory piece, then roll the strip up tightly over the chenille stem or pipe cleaner, forming a cylinder for the arms. Glue edge flat. Tie 1/2 in. from each end for hands and cut ends close.

For sleeves, bring edges of a 5-1/2-in. medium blue piece together to form a tube. Overlap edges 1/2 in. and glue together. Fit tube over arm cylinder, centering it and gathering center together.

Slide arm/sleeve piece between the front and back sections of the ivory body piece. Tie with thread below arms and cut thread ends close.

For undergarment, fold the two 12-in. medium blue strips diagonally over the shoulders as in Fig. 1, crossing the pieces in front. Glue the pieces together where they overlap. Tie around the waist and cut thread ends close.

For robe, make a 6-in. slit up the center of the 12-in. red piece. Bring the two narrower ends over the shoulders with the slit opening at center front and around neck. Smooth the piece down, overlap and glue side edges together below arms. Tie the piece of twine loosely around the waist and cut to desired length. Trim bottom edge so figure stands flat.

Cut a 6-in. length of dark brown doll hair, stretching it to be about 1 in. wide. Glue center of piece to top of head, pulling remainder of hair back and away from the face and gluing into place on head.

Cut a 3-in. length of dark brown doll hair for beard. Glue into position on chin.

Glue twig to one hand for staff.

Mary: Cut these pieces of paper twist: one 12-in. and one 6-in. piece of ivory, one 5-1/2-in. and two 12-in. pieces of light blue and one 12-in. piece of medium blue. Cut a 6-in. length of dark auburn doll hair.

Untwist pieces and follow directions for Joseph, except use light blue pieces for sleeves and undergarment, medium blue piece for robe and dark auburn doll hair. Omit twine, beard and staff.

Cut these pieces from untwisted paper twist: one 1-1/2-in.-wide x 3-in.-long piece of light blue and one 3-in.-wide x 4-in.-long piece of medium blue.

Tie around waist, cutting ends close. Overlap and glue front edges of robe together up to waist. Fold the 1-1/2-in.-wide x 3-in.-long light blue piece lengthwise in thirds to form a 1/2-in. x 3-in. cummerbund. Wrap around waist, with cut ends meeting in front and glue in place.

For veil, position the 3-in. x 4-in. medium blue piece on figure's head, centering long edge over front of hair. Form a fold on each side of head as in Fig. 2, trimming bottom of veil to a smoothly rounded edge and gluing in place.

Baby Jesus: Cut a 3-in. piece of ivory twist and a 4-in. piece of red twist and untwist them.

Place the 1/2-in. wooden bead in the center of the ivory twist. Twist the paper around the bead, smoothing out a face side. Tie the twist just below the bead to form head and body.

For the blanket, place baby diagonally on the red piece with head 1/4 in. from a corner. Glue end of red piece over the body, then glue each side edge over the body, leaving only the head visible.

ASSEMBLY: Apply glue to the bottom edge of Joseph's robe and glue him to the right side of the craft stick base.

Place baby in Mary's arms and glue in place. Fold Mary into kneeling position. Apply glue to lower portion of her robe which will touch base and glue her on the left side of base as shown in photo. Glue robe and undergarment layers together so they lie flat in back.

Glue small bunches of excelsior around the figures, covering up the craft stick base. ▲

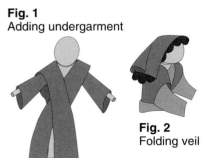

Fig. 1
Adding undergarment

Fig. 2
Folding veil

Readers' Poetry Corner

Christmas Album

The Christmas Days of long ago
Will always be a part
Of that precious picture album
I keep locked inside my heart.

Simple beauty in a manger
Lit by midnight candle flame,
I can hear the organ playing
Carols praising Jesus' name.

Children dressed as little angels,
Cherub faces all aglow,
While the bells atop the steeple
Sing their song across the snow.

Oh, the Christmas morning faces
Of a little girl and boy,
And the squeals of happy laughter
As they open each new toy.

The man I love, his smiling face,
Beneath the mistletoe…
The diamond ring he gave to me
One Christmas long ago.

Each Christmas Eve, beside the fire,
Those pictures are so clear—
The Christmas memories in my heart
Grow sweeter every year.
                    —**Dawn E. McCormick**
                       Spring, Texas

What Is Christmas?

It's more than just a special time
Of gay festivity,
Or packages all heaped beneath
The shimmering Christmas tree.

It's more than just a starry night
Or sleigh bells o'er the snow.
It's more than merry carolers
Or candlelight's soft glow.

It's peace and joy of lasting kind
The season does impart.
It's faith and hope, a whispered prayer—
Things felt deep in the heart.

It's glory that a Savior came
To earth from Heaven above.
It's God's most priceless gift to us—
A miracle of love.

                    —**Beverly J. Anderson**
                       Fort Lauderdale, Florida

Green Thumb Guarantees Holidays Are Berry Merry

EACH CHRISTMAS, Betty Dickinson makes local folks see red…and they love every minute of it.

Far from being angry at her, Betty's neighbors in the small western-North Carolina town of Hendersonville flock to the nursery where she tends some 50 varieties of holly. "The plants are just so beautiful when they're flush with new growth and loaded with berries," Betty says of the Christmas-colored crop she and her late husband began growing a decade ago.

Festive crimson berries *are* among the most familiar features of this seasonal plant. But take a stroll around Betty's acres and you're also likely to see berries in hues of bright yellow, orange and even black. The sizes and shapes of holly plants vary greatly, too—from shrubby Blue Holly to hybrids that shoot up to 6 or 7 feet tall.

Whatever the type, however, holly is anything but a hurry-up proposition. According to Betty, the span from start to sale can extend to half a dozen years.

The process begins by taking cuttings in late summer. Called "liners", they show roots in 4 to 8 weeks. Then they remain in their small pots through the winter.

Come spring, each little plant is moved into a liner bed. "With 1,500 plants a year here," Betty grins, "it makes

for lots of hands-and-knees work!"

The liners spend at least a year in their new home before they're planted in the field, usually in March or April. From then, it's another 3 to 5 years until the plants reach selling size.

All the same, Betty never tires of the lively holiday greenery. Even when she's not nurturing new plants or pruning larger shrubs for Christmas decoration makings, she surrounds herself with holly.

"I make long-lasting holly wreaths with an agent that keeps the leaves fresh," she notes. "I also collect all sorts of items with a holly motif—aprons, jewelry and glassware."

Her *favorite*, though? That's easy to select. "It's a hand-painted holly sweatshirt," she reveals, "with my grandchildren's names on the leaves!"

Editor's Note: *Betty welcomes visitors to Hollydale Nursery at 37 Blackjack Rd., Hendersonville NC 28739, but suggests a phone call first at 1-704/692-2861. For information on the Holly Society of America (of which Betty's a member), write to it at 11318 W. Murdock, Wichita KS 67212.* ▲

Fiction...

To Read a Christmas Quilt

By Roxana Chalmers of Sedalia, Colorado

FROM the cozy overstuffed chair—reserved for her out of respect for her 86 years—Rachel gazed fondly around at the Christmas Eve bustle. *This* is what she'd looked forward to for many months...everyone here at once, filling the old farmhouse with noise, love and laughter!

Over and over, though, she found her eyes settling on the two youngest members of her family. Great-grandchildren Sara, 6, and Tommy, 4, seemed the very essence of Christmas. How she would like to get to know them better—if only there was a way to bridge the wide gap of years between them.

That evening, after they'd said good night, Rachel wished she could read them bedtime stories the way she had all the other children. But her eyes tired so easily these days...

Suddenly, she noticed Sara and Tommy peeking through the doorway. "Hey, you two," scolded their mother. "You're supposed to be in bed."

"I can't sleep," Sara protested. "My tummy's too excited."

"Mine, too," Rachel piped up.

The children peered at their great-grandmother in amazement. "Are *you* thinking about Santa Claus, too?" Sara wondered.

"Oh yes," Rachel happily responded.

Sara looked earnest. "Can you read to us, Gran?" she asked.

Rachel began to explain why she couldn't—then had an idea. "Sure I can," she chirped, unfolding the quilt from the back of her chair. "And we don't even need a book!"

"We can't read a blanket!" Tommy giggled as he climbed onto the arm of her chair. Sara squeezed in beside her.

"Oh no?" Rachel smiled, sliding over. "Let's see."

She caressed a square of worn blue fabric. "This is from the dress of a china doll I got for Christmas the year I was 10."

"A Chinese doll?" Tommy wrinkled his forehead.

Rachel chuckled. "No, her head was china, like a dish."

"But that would break," Sara observed.

"You're right. One day, when my brothers and I were playing fireman, I dropped her from the attic window. Your Great-Granduncle Roy couldn't catch her."

"And her head broke?" blurted out Tommy, enthralled.

"Into smithereens."

"Did you get another doll?" Sara queried with concern.

"No, the next Christmas I got skates."

The two stared wide-eyed at Rachel. Their great-grandmother had once been a little girl?

Rachel pointed next to a square of embroidered flowers. "Here's another Christmas story—about a *real* fire."

"Were you playing fireman again?" Tommy quizzed gleefully.

"No," Rachel recalled, "but we almost needed one! Your grandfather was playing with his new steam engine under the table, and sparks set the tablecloth on fire."

"What did he do then?" Sara glanced toward the dining room.

"Well, he dumped the water glasses on the flames. Aunt Ruth grabbed the turkey so quickly it slid off the platter and across the floor. I rescued the gravy. And Uncle Roy got hold of the dish of mashed potatoes—his favorite part of the dinner!

"We had to bundle up the tablecloth and throw it out into the snow, still burning." Rachel touched the tiny stitched flowers. "Afterward, this is all that was left of it."

"Let's do another one!" Tommy leaned forward eagerly.

Rachel laughed, explaining, "They aren't *all* Christmas stories...and they aren't *all* that exciting."

Sara pointed to a triangle of white satin. "Is this from a wedding dress?"

"That's a good guess." Rachel smoothed the fabric. "But, no, it's from a christening dress. It was made for your uncle, and, I suppose, since he was born on Christmas Day..."

"A dress for a *boy*?" Tommy frowned.

"Yes—all the babies in our family have worn that dress. In fact, the last baby to wear it was you."

"It was?" Tommy gasped. "Did Cody wear it, too?" Clearly, he couldn't imagine his husky teenage cousin wearing a dress, even as a baby!

"Cody, too," Rachel assured him.

The stories went on, with the children taking turns choosing a quilt square and learning about their mother's first-day-of-school dress...Uncle John's lucky shirt...and Aunt Kate's strawberry-picking apron.

At last, Tommy's head drooped. "He's getting sleepy," whispered Sara.

"I'm feeling kind of sleepy myself," Rachel whispered back. "How about you, honey?"

"Yeah," she sighed. "But we didn't finish the quilt."

Rachel stroked Sara's silky blond curls. "We'll have time for the rest before you go home," she promised—refolding her quilt that, like a bridge, *had* carried her great-grandchildren across the generations. ▲

Christmas Country Style's BIG Occasion for Crafter

By C. Shaw of Kenedy, Texas

WHEN it comes to holiday decorating, Wysenda Fischer has her work cut out for her. The wooden Christmas scenes she crafts to enliven her rural Lone Star community of Yorktown definitely fit the spacious state's expansive acres!

Displayed at her parents' homestead, the spirit-brightening seasonal array appears as big as all Texas—one display alone extends more than *200 feet*.

There's a considerable dose of country behind those sizable Santas, sleighs and such besides. She and husband Billy raise cattle, Wysenda notes, and "I often think about my next project while I'm wrangling stock or plowing on the tractor."

This highly enthusiastic Christmas crafter got an early start on her cutting-edge hobby when she received a saber saw as a birthday present the year she turned 9.

"Then," she adds, "when I took woodworking as part of my FFA courses in high school, I quickly became the 'ideas' girl. I'd help my classmates make cupboards, shelves, director's chairs…all sorts of things."

These days, Wysenda's still getting an early start. With the holiday season fresh in her mind, she usually begins plotting her latest Christmas creations in January. Needless to say, she thinks *big*.

"The first thing I do is find my pattern and enlarge it," she details. "Then I cut it out of 1/2-inch signboard and paint it white. Next, I draw the pattern on the board and paint it."

Shortly after Thanksgiving, eager viewers come out for the woodwork. Cars travel her folks' country road day and night to take in Wysenda's holiday handiwork…and don't stop until after Christmas. "You can't miss it," she laughs.

Already, there are indications the eye-filling exhibition will go on long into the future. At age 3, daughter Wycoda is showing signs she's inherited more than a little of her mother's interest and ability. "When *I* paint," Wysenda smiles, "*she* paints."

But this country woman who loves the holidays in a large way has no thoughts of laying aside her band saw and paintbrush any time soon. "My newest scene," she reveals, "features 12 snowmen plus a gingerbread house." Sounds like *lots* of fun! ▲

WOODEN WONDERLAND. Lone Star artist Wysenda Fischer (below) crafts larger-than-life displays to spruce up parents' home at holidays.

Southerner's Sweet Crop Adds Spice to The Season

DECKING THE HALLS really grows on Sylvia Tippett. This country woman—who raises a bevy of beautiful herbs and flowers on her family's farm—rounds out each year by handcrafting unique holiday wreaths.

"We had a wonderful farm, but it needed an alternative crop," the Godwin, North Carolina widow recalls. "So I started an herb nursery and developed several culinary blends."

Some 15 years later, her harvest is a "blooming" business—featuring a retail shop, mail-order catalog, field row crops and display gardens with herbs intended for everything from seasoning food to keeping insects away!

Come Christmastime, that nature's bounty becomes the basis for Sylvia's well-rounded country creations. Sweet Annie, straw and silver king are combined with Brazilian red pepper berries, hydrangea, roses, strawflowers and other merry makings in her homegrown wreaths.

Her herbs are the main ingredient in seasonal swags, herbal bouquets and dried flower arrangements as well.

"Each Christmas, we come up with other items, too," Sylvia says. "Sometimes, the lack of a particular flower or herb inspires an idea. Then we wind up with a totally new and different look!"

Sylvia's tie to the 300-acre farm is anything but new, however. Currently known as Rasland Farm—the "Ras" comes from the initials of Rufus and Agnes, Sylvia's parents, plus their daughter—it's been in the family for five generations.

Today, filling orders from as far

away as Japan, family is very much involved. Sylvia's Aunt Dorothy is part of the crafty crew turning fragrant herbs into appealing accents. When she's not maintaining the farm's computer system or propagating plants in the greenhouses, daughter Jennifer follows in Sylvia's stylish steps by designing and crafting one-of-a-kind wreaths.

Son Jon, the farm's production manager, converted a 50-year-old barn into office space—complete with a loft for classes and demonstrations. His older brother, Jeffrey, and wife Lucinda edit the farm's brochures and catalogs.

So it's no wonder Sylvia smiles so often—for her, Christmas is a family occasion...365 days a year!

Editor's Note: *Sylvia's catalog is filled with wreaths, bouquets, dried herbs, plants and extracts and includes information on an annual Herb Fest. To request a copy, send $3 to Rasland Farm, NC 82 at US 13, Godwin NC 28344. The phone number is 1-910/ 567-2705.* ▲

HER WREATHS MAKE SCENTS. Herb grower Sylvia Tippett (at top right) fashions festive wreaths from fragrant flora.

Encounter with a Little Star Changed Wise Man's Course!

By Lee Stoops of Norwalk, Ohio

It's long been said that Christmas is for children. The year she was 2 years old, our daughter Bonnie underscored the point—in a most unexpected way.

Our family belonged to a small rural congregation with a wonderful pastor. Pastor Harper and his wife had five children, and that had helped him develop tremendous patience and powers of concentration. No distraction, it seemed, could disturb him once he started "sermonizing".

This particular year, we looked forward to a very special Christmas Eve. Because he was leading two other congregations as well, Pastor Harper decided to combine the evening service for all three and hold it at one of the larger churches.

When we arrived there that night, we were immediately struck by how different it was from our church. Newly remodeled, it didn't have the traditional feel we were used to.

We soon noticed something else—three congregations celebrating together was making for a tight fit even in the more spacious quarters! With both Bonnie *and* her 5-year-old sister, Michelle, along with us, we were running a little late. So we were ushered to the only remaining space available—"Deacon's Row"...the very first pew!

Settling in our seats, we tried not to feel too self-conscious. But our little cherubs weren't going to make that easy.

Normally, before the collection plate was passed, they'd curl up by my side and drift off to sleep. Here, however, the bright fluorescent bulbs overhead all but ruled out the possibility of naps.

Sure enough, midway through the pastor's sermon on "The Other Wise Man", Bonnie began to wriggle and squirm. Hoping to quiet her restlessness, I gave her my purse to explore. And that was the first step in sending the entire church into an uproar!

You see, Bonnie was facing toward the congregation. Because of that, my husband and I didn't notice the treasure she'd plucked from my purse—a pair of *sunglasses*.

Without skipping a beat, our little star donned the glasses, curtseyed from her seat beside Dad...and brought the house down with a winsome smile of complete innocence.

"The Other Wise Man" became a tradition at Christmas Eve service from that evening on. But Pastor Harper proved he was the *fifth* wise man. He never again read from a typed text, and he gave only a short summary of the Christmas story.

What's more, he called on another well-known and beloved Bible story for inspiration. Dubbing the seats far in the back of the church "The Inn", he made sure there was always plenty of room there for latecomers—and for families like ours with budding young Christmas stars! ▲

Underneath the Tree

Christmas is a magic time
For little girls and boys...
The colored lights, the ornaments,
Old Santa Claus, new toys.

But when I was a little girl,
The grandest thing to me—
Each night when I was dressed for bed,
I'd lie beneath the tree.

The fragrant boughs above my head
Adorned with baubles bright,
With popcorn chains and candy canes,
With green and crimson light.

And as I lay beneath the tree,
I'd dream of Christmas Day,
Of all the wondrous toys and games
To come on Santa's sleigh.

All grown up, a mother now,
The dearest sight to see—
My little ones all dressed for bed,
Asleep beneath the tree.

—**Dawn E. McCormick**
Spring, Texas

Craft Section...
Delightful Doll's Cute As a Button

TICKLE a daughter's, granddaughter's or niece's fancy with this darling doll that's right on the button.

Rosalie Sheptick of Hayward, Wisconsin "strung up" this quick and easy idea for making use of the stray buttons we all collect. Dress one little lady in a festive holiday frock...then craft a spare in colors to match that special girl's room year-round!

Materials:

1-3/4-inch wooden ball knob for head
3-3/4-inch crocheted doll hat
Large (1-1/2 inches wide x 2 inches long) thread spool for body
Four small (1/2-inch x 1/2-inch) spools
Heavy thread or elastic, four 15-inch lengths
About 67 flat buttons, sizes and colors of your choice
Print fabric scraps—2-1/2-inch x 12-inch piece for dress, 2-1/4-inch circle for covering spool and 3/4-inch x 17-inch piece for hatband
3/4 yard of coordinating 1/8-inch-wide ribbon for tie
12 inches of 1-1/4-inch-wide pre-gathered eyelet lace for bottom of dress
Maxi-curl doll hair
Glue gun and glue sticks
Matching thread
Hand-sewing needle
Scissors
Standard sewing supplies (optional)
Light pink acrylic craft paint
Medium paintbrush
Fine-line permanent black and red markers

Directions:
BODY: Paint wooden ball knob (head) with light pink. Let dry. Referring to photo, add face with black and red markers.

Cut 1-in. to 1-1/2-in. strands of doll hair and glue to cover head top, sides and back. Also glue on curls to hang down in back. Glue hat on back of head. Let dry.

For arms, string buttons and spools onto the 15-in. pieces of elastic or heavy thread as follows: Thread elastic or heavy thread down through one hole in the first nine buttons, then thread through center of one small spool. Thread six more buttons onto the elastic or heavy thread. Go back through a second hole in each button and through center of small spool to top of arm. Tie ends together in a knot. Set aside. Make the other arm in the same manner, being sure to add enough buttons to make both arms the same length.

For legs, use the same technique as the arms, only string eight buttons, then add a small spool. Add eight more buttons, then go back through second hole in each button and through center of small spool. Tie ends together in a knot at top of leg. Set aside and put together the other leg in the same manner.

Tie the arms around the top of the large spool, allowing them to extend on opposite sides of doll. Tie the legs around the bottom of the large spool, so both hang down in front of doll. Trim off excess elastic or heavy thread. For added support, add a bead of glue over the elastic or heavy thread on the spool. Let dry.

DRESS: Glue the 2-1/4-in. circle of print fabric to the top of the spool. Fold the edges down over the sides of the spool, trimming the sides of the circle over each arm and gluing all edges into place. Let dry.

Glue the head centered on top of the fabric-covered spool, making sure she's facing toward the front (the side that the legs are hanging from). Let dry.

Press one long edge of the 2-1/2-in. x 12-in. dress piece under 1/4 in. Overlap folded edge of dress over gathered edge of eyelet lace and glue or edge-stitch the lace to the bottom edge of the dress piece. Fold dress piece in half crosswise and sew or glue the short ends of the dress together 1/4 in. from the edge to make a tube.

Make a running stitch 1/8 in. from the remaining long edge of the dress piece (see Fig. 1). Fit around doll body and pull up gathers to fit below arms around body, 1/4 in. from top of spool in front and at top edge of spool in back. Tie securely under arms and glue in place.

HAT: Fold the 3/4-in. x 17-in. piece of print fabric lengthwise in thirds, forming a 1/4-in.-wide strip for hatband. Glue hatband to base of hat crown, crossing ends at center back so they extend evenly. Let dry. Trim ends diagonally. Glue a large button on the spot where the ribbon crosses. Then glue a small button centered on top of the large button and a small button on each side of it. Let dry. Glue hat to back of doll's head.

FINISHING: Tie ribbon around doll's neck with a bow at center front. Let the ribbon ends hang down, trimming ends diagonally. Glue two buttons down the dress front, centering them 1/4 in. apart. Let dry. ▲

Fig. 1
Running stitch

Each square on the chart equals one stitch. Use the colors indicated on the color key to complete the cross-stitching, then backstitching as in Fig. 1.

Begin stitching the words MERRY CHRISTMAS, with lower edge of stitching 1 in. above the brim, working from center seam of cap out. Loosely cross-stitch over the canvas using a sharp needle. Make sure the stitches are even by making the stitches in the center of the large holes of the canvas. When starting and stopping threads, be sure to knot the ends on the wrong side of the cap.

When the design is complete, remove the basting threads and trim the canvas to about 1/2 in. from the stitching. Lightly moisten the canvas and use tweezers to pull the individual canvas threads out from under the stitching. Let dry. ▲

Fig. 1

Cross-Stitch   Backstitch

Cheery Cap Is the Perfect Way to Top Off Holiday

JUMP into the season "headfirst"... by crafting this clever counted cross-stitch cap for someone you love.

Renee Dent of Conrad, Montana shares the design for the holiday hat. It's perfect for an off-duty Santa who's set to spread some Christmas cheer.

Materials Needed:
Chart on this page
6-inch x 6-inch square of 14-count waste canvas
DMC six-strand embroidery floss in colors listed on color key
Red baseball-style cap
Embroidery needle
Scissors
Masking tape
Tweezers
Straight pins
Sewing thread

Finished Size: Design area of Merry Christmas Cap is 66 stitches wide x 43 stitches high. Design area measures 4-3/4 inches wide by 3-1/8 inches high on 14-count canvas.

Directions:
Tape edges of waste canvas to prevent fraying. Find the center of the cap. Position the bottom of the waste canvas level with the inner edge of the brim of the cap, centered from side to side. Pin waste canvas to cap and baste into place, working from the top down. Remove pins.

Find the center of the chart by joining the arrows from top to bottom of chart. Separate six-strand floss and use three strands for all cross-stitching and two strands for all backstitching.

"MERRY CHRISTMAS" CAP
COLOR KEY   **DMC**
⊛ White
■ Christmas Red 321
⬛ Pearl Gray 415
◉ Very Light Brown 435
⊠ Light Tan 437
⊠ Medium Topaz 725
⊙ Light Topaz 726
∞ Medium Pink 776
◰ Medium Dark Emerald Green . . 911
⬛ Light Pink Beige 951
⬛ Black Brown 3371
BACKSTITCHING
╱ Black Brown 3371

"MERRY CHRISTMAS" CHART

Crafty Christmas Combs Dress Up Festive Tresses

THESE BEADED BEAUTIES can be the crowning touch for your holiday hairdo. But don't stop there!

Renee Dent of Conrad, Montana recommends crafting her counted bead combs for all the ladies on your list. "They make wonderful gifts for daughters, sisters, mothers and friends," she notes, "and they can be worn with any holiday outfit."

Materials Needed for two:
Chart on this page
One 2-inch x 4-inch piece of ivory 14-count perforated plastic
Two 1/2-inch x 2-3/4-inch pieces of white felt
Ecru six-strand embroidery floss
Seed beads in colors listed on color key*
Size 26 tapestry needle
Two 2-1/2-inch-wide plastic hair combs
Scissors
Tacky (white) glue

*Renee used Mill Hill Seed Beads, avail-

able in most craft stores. To find a store that carries the beads in your area, write to Mill Hill, P.O. Box 1060, Janesville WI 53547; 1-800/447-1332.

Finished Size: Finished design size is 1/2 inch wide x 2-3/4 inches long. Design area is 5 stitches high x 35 stitches wide.

Directions:
Cut a 30-in. piece of ecru six-strand floss and use a doubled strand for all stitching. Fold this strand in half and thread both cut ends through the needle.

Referring to chart, attach beads individually. To begin stitching, secure the first bead with a half cross-stitch in the upper left corner of the perforated plastic, 1/2 in. from each edge as follows: From under the perforated plastic, bring the needle up through the first hole, the lower left of the stitch, allowing the loop end of the floss to extend out on the wrong side. Pick up a bead with the tip of the needle, then go down into the second hole, the upper right of the stitch as in Fig. 1. As you do this, go through the loop of floss underneath the perforated plastic. Pull tightly.

Continue to add beads using half cross-stitches until pattern is complete. To end a strand and begin the next, run the tails of the floss under the stitches on the back of the perforated plastic.

Carefully trim away excess canvas, leaving one bar outside of beaded stitching for whipstitching. Round off sharp corners.

Secure the floss to the remaining bar on any edge of the design by following the directions for securing the first bead, making a stitch without adding a bead. Add a bead with each remaining stitch along each edge of each design.

Repeat in opposite corner of perforated plastic piece for second hair comb.

Glue each design onto a piece of the white felt and allow to dry. Glue a finished design onto the upper edge of each hair comb; let dry completely before wearing. ▲

Fig. 1
Beaded half cross-stitch

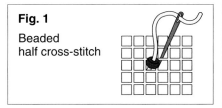

HAIR COMBS COLOR KEY — Mill Hill Seed Beads

▒ Gray	....	00150
✳ White	....	00479
▨ Victorian Gold	....	02011
■ Red Red	....	02013
▲ Creme de Mint	....	02020

HAIR COMBS CHART

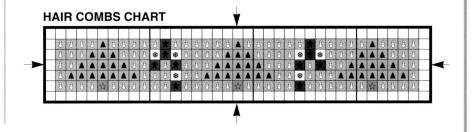

Craft Section...

His & Hers Vests Add Vivid Style To Season

YOUR favorite couple can cozy up to Christmas with this pair of bright vests!

Frances Hughes, Longview, Texas, fashioned this fun and festive design to add a dash of color to any holiday wardrobe. Grab your needles and knit up a gift that's sure to bring warm feelings all season long!

Materials Needed (for each vest):

Chunky yarn in 3-1/2-ounce skeins (100-gram/186-yard): for man's vest—three skeins of green and one skein of both red and white; for woman's vest—three skeins of red and one skein of both green and white*

Straight knitting needles—sizes 9 (5.5mm) and 10 (6mm) or sizes needed to obtain correct gauge

Two stitch holders

Yarn needle

Scissors

* Frances used Knitting Fever's Tivili Chunky yarn (100% acrylic yarn) in No. 425 Green, No. 436 Red and No. 431 White.

Gauge: In St st with larger needles and chunky yarn, 6-1/2 sts and 11 rows = 2 inches.

Finished Size: Man's vest has a garment chest measurement of 41 inches and back length of 23 inches. Woman's vest has a garment chest measurement of 34 inches and back length of 21-1/2 inches.

Notes/Stitches Used:

DOUBLE SEED STITCH: DS st
Row 1: (K 2, p 2) to last 2 sts, k 2.
Rows 2-3: (P 2, k 2) to last 2 sts, p 2.
Row 4: Repeat Row 1.
Repeat these four rows for pattern.

KNIT 1, PURL 1 RIBBING: K 1, p 1 ribbing
Every Row: * K 1, p 1, repeat from * across row.

SEED STITCH: Seed st
Row 1: K 1, p 1.
Row 2: P 1, k 1.
Repeat Rows 1 and 2.

STOCKINETTE STITCH: St st
Row 1 (RS): Knit.
Row 2 (WS): Purl.
Repeat Rows 1 and 2.

Directions:

MAN'S FRONT (MF): With smaller needles and green, cast on 70 sts.

MF Rows 1-12: Work in k 1, p 1 ribbing as follows: 2 rows green, 2 rows white, 4 rows red, 2 rows white, 2 rows green.

MF Rows 13-26: With green and larger needles, work in St st.

MF Rows 27-28: Knit with white.

MF Row 29: (K 1 green, p 1 red) across. Fasten off green.

MF Row 30: With red, purl.

MF Rows 31-38: Work DS st across.

MF Rows 39-40: With white, work in St st.

MF Row 41: With green, knit.

MF Row 42: P 3, k 1, * p 8, k 1, repeat from * to last 3 sts, p 3.

MF Row 43: K 2, p 3, * k 6, p 3, repeat from * to last 2 sts, k 2.

MF Row 44: P 1, * k 5, p 4, repeat from * to last st, p 1.

MF Row 45: P 7, * k 2, p 7 * across.

MF Row 46: Repeat MF Row 44.
MF Row 47: Repeat MF Row 43.
MF Rows 48-51: Repeat MF Rows 42-45.
MF Row 52: Repeat MF Row 44.
MF Row 53: Repeat MF Row 43.
MF Row 54: Repeat MF Row 42.
MF Row 55: Repeat MF Row 41. Fasten off green.
MF Row 56: With white, purl.
MF Row 57: Knit. Fasten off white.
MF Row 58: With red, purl.
MF Rows 59-66: Work in DS st.
MF Row 67: Repeat MF Row 29.
MF Rows 68-69: With white, knit.
MF Row 70: With green, purl.
Underarm Shaping: MF Row 71: With green, bind off 5 sts, knit to end: 65 sts.
MF Row 72: Bind off 5 sts, purl to end: 60 sts.
MF Rows 73-82: Work in St st.
MF Rows 83-87: Work in Seed st.
MF Rows 88-98: Work in St st.
Neck Shaping: MF Row 99: P 22, place next 16 sts on st holder, attach a second ball of yarn, p 22.
MF Row 100: Purl.
MF Rows 101-104: For left shoulder, work Seed st to last 2 sts before neck opening, k 2 together in back of st; for right shoulder, k 2 together, work Seed st to end of row.

Continuing to keep in Seed st pattern and working both shoulders simultaneously, dec 1 st each side of neck opening as in Row 101 on next right side row: 20 sts on each side of neck opening.

MF Rows 105-110: Work in St st, dec 1 st each side of neck opening on right side rows five more times: 15 sts each.

MF Rows 111-114: Work in St st.

MF Rows 115: Bind off.

MAN'S BACK (MB): With smaller needles and green, cast on 70 sts.

MB Rows 1-12: Repeat MF Rows 1-12.

MB Rows 13-70: Work in St st.

MB Rows 71-72: Repeat MF Rows 71-72 for underarm shaping.

MB Rows 73-114: Work in St st.

MB Row 115: Bind off first 15 sts; knit, then place next 30 sts on st holder, bind off remaining 15 sts.

Sew front to back at left shoulder.

NECK RIBBING: Row 1: With white, k 30 sts from back st holder, pick up and knit 20 sts down side front, k 16 sts from front st holder, pick up and knit 20 sts up other side front: 86 sts.

Rows 2-8: Work in k 1, p 1 ribbing as follows: 1 row white, 2 rows red, 2 rows white, 2 rows green. Bind off in pattern.

SLEEVE RIBBING: Row 1: With red, pick up and knit 73 sts from front underarm to back underarm (bound-off sts to bound-off sts).

Rows 2-6: Work in k 1, p 1 ribbing as follows: 1 row red, 2 rows white, 2 rows green. Bind off in pattern.

Repeat Rows 1-6 for second sleeve.

Sew right shoulder and both side seams, stitching ends of sleeve ribbing to bound-off sts of front and back.

Lay out flat, cover with a damp cloth and allow to dry.

WOMAN'S FRONT (WF): With red and smaller needles, cast on 60 sts.

WF Rows 1-10: Work k 1, p 1 ribbing as follows: 2 rows red, 2 rows white, 4 rows green, 2 rows white.

WF Rows 11-24: With red and larger needles, work in St st.

WF Rows 25-26: With white, knit.

WF Row 27: (K 1 red, p 1 green) across. Fasten off green.

WF Row 28: With green, purl.

WF Rows 29-34: Work DS st with green.

WF Rows 35-36: With white, work in St st, inc 1 st on WF Row 35: 61 sts.

WF Rows 37-51: With red, repeat MF Rows 41-55. Fasten off red.

WF Row 52: With white, purl.

WF Row 53: Knit, dec 1: 60 sts. Fasten off white.

WF Row 54: With green, purl.

WF Rows 55-60: Work DS st.

WF Row 61: Repeat WF Row 27.

WF Row 62-63: With white, knit.

WF Row 64: With red, bind off 5 sts, purl to end: 55 sts.

WF Row 65: Bind off 5 sts, knit to end: 50 sts.

WF Rows 66-74: Work in St st.

WF Rows 75-79: Work in Seed st.

WF Row 80: Purl.

WF Rows 81-88: Work in St st.

Neck Shaping: WF Row 89: Work in Seed st on first 19 sts, place next 12 sts on holder; attach second ball of yarn, work last 19 sts in Seed st.

WF Rows 90-93: Work in Seed st on both shoulders simultaneously, decreasing on right side rows (Rows 91 and 93) as follows: For left shoulder, continue working in Seed st to last 2 sts before neck opening, k 2 together in back of st; for right shoulder, k 2 together, work in Seed st to end of row.

WF Row 94: Purl.

WF Rows 95-99: Work in St st on both shoulders simultaneously, dec 1 st each side of neck opening as in Row 91 on right side rows three more times: 14 sts on each side.

WF Rows 100-109: Work in St st. Bind off remaining sts.

WOMAN'S BACK (WB): With smaller needles and red, cast on 60 sts.

WB Rows 1-10: Repeat WF Rows 1-10.

WB Rows 11-68: Work in St st.

WB Rows 69-70: Repeat WF Rows 64-65 for underarm shaping

WB Rows 71-108: Work in St st.

WB Row 109: Bind off first 14 sts; knit, then place next 22 sts on st holder, bind off remaining 14 sts.

Sew front to back at left shoulder.

NECK RIBBING: Row 1: With white, k 22 sts from back st holder, pick up and knit 20 sts down side front, k 12 sts from front st holder, pick up and knit 20 sts up other side front: 74 sts.

Rows 2-8: Work in k 1, p 1 ribbing as follows: 1 row of white, 2 rows green, 2 rows white, 2 rows red. Bind off in pattern.

SLEEVE RIBBING: Row 1: With green, pick up and knit 68 sts from front underarm to back underarm (from bound-off sts to bound-off sts).

Rows 2-5: Work in k 1, p 1 ribbing as follows: 1 row green, 2 rows white, 2 rows red. Bind off in pattern.

Repeat Rows 1-5 for second sleeve.

Sew right shoulder and both side seams, stitching ends of sleeve ribbing to bound-off sts of front and back.

Lay out flat, cover with a damp cloth and allow to dry. ▲

ABBREVIATIONS:

dec	decrease
DS st	Double Seed stitch
inc	increase
k	knit
p	purl
st(s)	stitch(es)
St st	Stockinette stitch

Holiday Tip...
Bigger Isn't Always Better in Choosing a Tree

LIKE many families, we hunt for the *perfect* Christmas tree to put in our living room each year. But we also start a second search—for the "runt of the litter"!

Why? After remodeling my country kitchen, I discovered that a smaller, scragglier tree would go perfectly with my new rustic decor.

The "good tree" gets all of the special ornaments I've collected over the years, along with the handmade ones that our Justin, 9, and Heather, 7, have brought home from school.

But my country kitchen tree has a more relaxed look. It's decked out with red raffia bows, old-fashioned paper ornaments, candy canes, gingerbread cookies and candles (unlit, of course!). Our two youngsters have a great time

decorating this tree. It's just their size!
—*Sue Gronholz*
Columbus, Wisconsin

Finished Size: Stocking is about 22 inches long.

Gauge: When working in St st, 18 sts and 22 rows = 4 inches.

KNITTING REMINDERS:
Changing colors: To avoid holes when changing colors, always pick up new color yarn from beneath the dropped yarn.
Working in rounds: Place sts on 3 dp needles. Place a marker at beginning of round, moving marker with each round worked. Being careful not to twist sts, join last st to first st by pulling up yarn firmly and knitting first st with fourth needle for first knit st.
Stockinette stitch: St st
   Row 1 (RS): Knit
   Row 2 (WS): Purl
   Repeat Rows 1 and 2.
   Rounds: Knit every round.
K 2, p 2 ribbing:
   Every Row: (K 2, p 2) across row.

Directions:
With straight knitting needles and A, cast on 60 sts.
   Rows 1-8: Work in k 2, p 2 ribbing, inc 1 st at end of Row 8: 61 sts.
   Rows 9-10: With C, work in St st.
   Rows 11-12: With A, work in St st.
   Rows 13-22: Follow Joy Chart for these rows. Starting at the bottom of the chart, read from right to left for a knit row, from left to right for a purl row using colors listed on color key.
   Rows 23-24: With A, work in St st.
   Rows 25-26: With C, work in St st.
   Rows 27-30: Repeat Rows 23-26.
   Rows 31-34: With B, work in St st.
   Rows 35-65: Follow Wreath Chart for these rows as instructed for Joy chart; at the same time, begin on Row 51 and every fourth row thereafter to dec 1 st at beginning and end of each row four times: 53 sts at end of Row 63.
   Rows 66-70: With B, work in St st, beginning with a WS row.
   Rows 71-76: Repeat Rows 25-30.
   Rows 77-80: With A, work in St st.
   Top of foot: Row 81: K 40, slip last 13 sts on small holder for heel.
   Row 82: P 27, slip last 13 sts on second small holder for heel.
   Rows 83-95: St st with C on 27 sts, dec 1 st at end of Row 95; slip remaining 26 sts onto a large holder.
   HEEL: Heel Rows 1-11: Slip the first 13 sts from the holder onto a dp needle, slip the second group of 13 sts onto the same dp needle so that the ends of the row are at middle of needle. With right side facing, join C and work 11 rows in St st ending with a RS row.

This Nifty Knit Stocking
Will Make Mantels Merry

HERE'S one Christmas stocking that'll fit the big occasion at your house! Louise Purpura of Valparaiso, Indiana designed her stocking large enough to stuff with *tons* of Yuletide treasures.

Materials Needed:
Charts on next page
Worsted-weight yarn in 4-ounce (115-gram) skeins—one each of red (A), white (B) and green (C)
Knitting needles—pair of straight and set (four needles) of double-pointed in size 8 (5mm) or size needed to obtain correct gauge
Stitch holders—two small and one large
Stitch marker
Size C/2 (2.75/3mm) crochet hook
Tapestry needle
Scissors
1/2 yard of lining fabric
Matching thread
Small jingle bell (optional)
Standard sewing supplies

Turning Heel: Heel Row 12: P 15, p 2 tog, p 1, turn.

Heel Row 13: Sl 1, k 5, sl 1, k 1, psso, k 1, turn.

Heel Row 14: Sl 1, p 6, p 2 tog, p 1, turn.

Heel Row 15: Sl 1, k 7, sl 1, k 1, psso, k 1, turn.

Heel Row 16: Sl 1, p 8, p 2 tog, p 1, turn.

Heel Rows 17-22: Continue in this manner, working out toward sides of heel and always having 1 more st before each dec on every row until 16 sts remain. Cut yarn.

Heel Row 23: Join C at top right-hand side of heel: Pick up and knit 12 sts along side of heel, k 16 sts of heel, pick up and k 12 sts along remaining side of heel: 40 sts.

Heel Row 24: Purl.

Heel Row 25: K 1, sl 1, k 1, psso, k to last 3 sts, k 2 tog, k 1: 38 sts.

Heel Rows 26-37: Repeat Rows 24 and 25: 26 sts at end of Row 37. Sl last 13 sts just worked from straight needle onto a dp needle. Cut yarn.

FOOT: Round 1: (See knitting reminders above for working in rounds.) With A and first needle, k 26 top of foot sts from large holder; second needle, k 13 heel sts from straight needle; third needle, k 13 heel sts from dp needle: 52 sts. Move marker with each round worked.

Rounds 2-14: Knit.

Toe shaping: Round 15: On first needle (top of foot), k 1, sl 1, k 1, psso, k to last 3 sts, k 2 tog, k 1; on second needle, k 1, sl 1, k 1, psso, k to end of needle; on third needle, k to last 3 sts, k 2 tog, k 1.

Round 16: Knit. Cut yarn.

Rounds 17-33: Repeat Rounds 15 and 16 until 4 sts remain on second and third needles: 16 sts. Cut yarn, leaving a 12-in. end. Draw yarn through remaining 16 stitches, pull tight and weave in end.

FINISHING: Sew back seam with B and sides of heel with C. Weave in all ends.

Hanging Loop: Using any color, ch 27. Fasten off, leaving an 8-in. yarn end. Fold chain in half and use yarn end to stitch both ends of chain to back seam at top edge of stocking.

Lining: Lay knitted stocking on fabric. Cut around stocking 1/2 in. from all edges. With right sides together, machine-stitch 1/2 in. from edges, leaving top edge open.

Fold top edge 2 in. to wrong side. Trim to 1/2 in. from fold. With lining wrong side out, put inside stocking, positioning the top edge of lining 1-1/2 in. from top edge of stocking and pushing lining toe down to stocking toe. Add jingle bell between layers, working it down into the toe. Use matching thread to hand-stitch top edge in place. ▲

STOCKING COLOR KEY
■ Red (A)
□ White (B)
▨ Green (C)
STRAIGHT STITCHES
✎ Red (A)

Fig. 1 Straight stitch

JOY CHART

22

Row 13

WREATH CHART

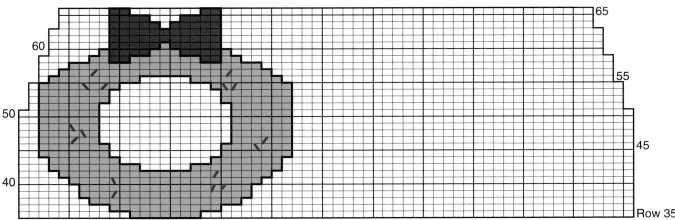

65
60
55
50
45
40
Row 35

Ferns Will Help You Wrap Up Your Yuletide Festively

THINK "brown paper packages tied up with string"...then try this crafty country variation on that tried-and-true standard!

Joanna Randolph Rott of Fort Washington, Pennsylvania came up with this idea for turning ordinary freezer paper or old grocery bags into custom-made gift wrap for all of your holiday packages. And make sure you save the scraps from your wrapping projects. You can use them to cut out matching tags to complete the look.

Materials Needed (for gift wrap):
Three or four fern fronds, natural
  or artificial
White freezer paper or brown paper
  grocery bags (plain side)
Newspapers or drop cloth
Green spray paint*

Scissors
Ribbon or yarn

*Joanna used Plasti-Kote Green Spray Paint.

Directions:
If using fresh ferns, cut them a day ahead and allow to dry flat between newspapers.

Be sure to read the instructions on paint can before beginning the project. Spread newspapers or drop cloth over your work area and adjacent areas to keep them clean.

Cut freezer paper or grocery bag to fit the gift box you're wrapping. Lay the paper on top of newspaper and either place heavy objects on the edges or tape them down to hold paper in place.

Randomly place the fern fronds on one end of the paper. Spray the area

with 2 to 3 coats of paint, moving the can in a circular motion. Let dry for 3 to 5 minutes.

Move the ferns to another part of the paper and follow directions as above. Repeat these steps until the paper is covered with a fern design. Let dry completely.

Wrap your gift box and tie with ribbon or yarn. Create variations using different colors of paint and paper.

Materials Needed (for tags):
Fern-stenciled gift wrap scraps (see
  above)
3-inch x 5-inch index cards
Ruler
Paper punch
Scissors
Pinking shears (optional)
Thick tacky glue*
Red yarn

*Joanna used Velverette Thick and Tacky Glue.

Directions:
RECTANGLE CARD: Cut a 3-3/4-in. x 5-3/4-in. piece from the scrap of stenciled gift wrap, using pinking shears if desired. Glue the index card centered on the piece of stenciled gift wrap. Fold in short ends of gift wrap even with edge of index card and glue in place.

Finishing: Let dry, then fold in half with index card inside.

Punch a hole in the upper left corner of the tag through all layers. Thread a 12-in. piece of yarn through hole and tie into a bow.

TREE CARD: Fold a 4-in. x 6-1/4-in. scrap of stenciled gift wrap in half. Lightly mark a 3-in.-wide x 2-1/2-in.-tall tree shape with a 1/4-in. x 1/2-in. trunk, leaving a 1/2-in. fold at top. Cut out, using pinking shears if desired.

Repeat to lightly mark an inner tree shape on a folded index card, omitting trunk and making the inner tree 1/4 in. smaller on bottom and side edges than gift wrap tree. Use scissors to cut shape from a folded index card. Glue inner tree centered on outer tree, matching folds as in Fig. 1.

Finishing: Finish as directed for Rectangle card, punching hole at center top of tree as shown in Fig. 1. ▲

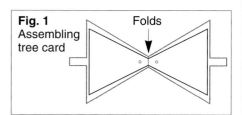

Fig. 1 Assembling tree card   Folds

Christmas Doily Branches Out with Rounds of Cheer

EVER WISH for evergreens that truly do stay ever green inside the house? Designer Emma Willey of Winston, Oregon has crocheted up this brightly beaded solution—a Christmas tree doily that's sure to take root and grow into a holiday favorite year after year!

Materials Needed:
Size 10 crochet cotton, 325-yard balls of both white and green
Small amount of both red crochet cotton and fine gold metallic cord
Size 6 (1.6mm) steel crochet hook
Small safety pin
Tapestry needle
Scissors
Green sewing thread
Hand-sewing needle
120-144 seed beads in assorted colors

Finished Size: Doily measures about 15 inches across.

Gauge: 8 dc = 1 inch.

Special Abbreviations:
2 SC CLUSTER (2 ScCl): Insert hook in next sp, yo, draw loop through, insert hook in following sp, yo, draw loop through, yo, draw through 3 loops on hook.
SHELL (Sh): 2 dc, ch 2, 2 dc.
SHELL IN SHELL (Sh in Sh): Work Sh in ch-2 sp of next sh.

Directions:
Note: As a marker, place a small safety pin in the first st of round, moving it to the first st of each succeeding round as work proceeds.
GOLD CENTER: With gold metallic cord, ch 8, join in the first ch to form a ring.
Round 1: Ch 4 (counts as first dc and ch 1), (dc in ring, ch 1) 23 times, end with sl st in third ch of beginning ch-4: 24 dc.
Round 2: Sl st into first ch-1 sp, * ch 3, sc in next ch-1 sp, repeat from * around, end with sl st in first ch of beginning ch-3. Fasten off.
TREES: Make eight trees, one every third sp as follows:
Row 1: With center wrong side up, attach green with sl st in any ch-3 sp, ch 3 (counts as dc), 2 dc in same sp: 3 dc.
Row 2: Ch 5, turn, 2 dc in base of ch-

5, dc in next 2 dc: 4 dc.
Row 3: Ch 5, turn, 2 dc in base of ch-5, dc in next 3 dc: 5 dc.
Rows 4-13: Beginning with ch-5, turn, work 2 dc in base of ch-5, dc in each remaining dc in each row: 15 dc in Row 13. Fasten off.

For second through eighth trees: Skip next 2 ch-3 sps and repeat Rows 1-13 for each tree. Do not turn after Row 13 of last tree.

OUTER ROUNDS: Round 1: Working around 3 outside edges of each tree, join white with sl st in ch-5 sp of Row 12 of any tree, * (ch 5, sc in next ch-5 sp) five times, ch 5, 2 ScCl between 2 gold ch-3 sps between trees; on next tree, (ch 5, sc in next ch-5 sp) six times, ch 5, sc in same sp, ch 5, sc in center dc of Row 13, ch 5, sc in sp between last 2 dc, ch 5, sc in next ch-5 sp, repeat from * around; omitting last sc, end with sl st in first ch of beginning ch-5.
Round 2: Sl st into center of next sp, * ch 6, sc in next sp, ch 3, sc in corresponding sp of next tree, (ch 6, sc in next sp) 6 times, repeat from * around; omitting last sc, end with sl st in first ch of beginning ch-6.
Round 3: Sl st back into center of last ch-6 of Round 2, * ch 8, skip 3 sps, sc in next sp, (ch 8, sc in next sp) 4 times, repeat from * around; omitting last (ch 8, sc in next sp), end with ch 4, tr in same st as beginning sl st.
Round 4: (Ch 8, sc in next sp) around, end with ch 4, tr in first ch of beginning ch-8.
Round 5: (Ch 3, dc, ch 2, 2 dc) in same sp made by ch-4 and tr of Round 4, ch 6, * (2 dc, ch 2, 2 dc) for Sh in next sp, ch 6, repeat from * around, end with sl st in top of beginning ch-3.
Round 6: Sl st into first ch-2 sp, (ch 3, dc, ch 2, 2 dc) in same sp, ch 6, * Sh in Sh, ch 6, repeat from * around, end with sl st in top of beginning ch-3.
Round 7: Sl st into first ch-2 sp, (ch 3, dc, ch 2, 2 dc) in same sp, ch 4, sc over next ch sps of Rounds 5 and 6, ch 4, * Sh in Sh, ch 4, sc over next ch sps of Rounds 5 and 6, ch 4, repeat from * around, end with sl st in top of beginning ch-3.
Round 8: Sl st into first ch sp, (ch 3, dc, ch 2, 2 dc) in same sp, ch 7, * Sh in Sh, ch 7, repeat from * around, end with sl st in top of beginning ch-3.
Round 9: Repeat Round 8. Fasten

off white.
Round 10: Join red with sl st in ch-2 sp of any Sh, (ch 3, dc, ch 2, 2 dc) in same sp, ch 5, sc over next ch sps of Rounds 8 and 9, ch 5, * Sh in Sh, ch 5, sc over next ch sps of Rounds 8 and 9, ch 5, repeat from * around, end with sl st in top of beginning ch-3. Fasten off red.
Round 11: Join gold metallic cord with sl st in ch-2 sp of any Sh, (sc, ch 3, sc) in same sp, * (ch 3, sc in next sp) twice, ch 3, (sc, ch 3, sc) in ch-2 sp of next Sh, repeat from * around, end with sl st in first ch of beginning ch-3. Fasten off gold.
FINISHING: Weave in all thread ends.

With green sewing thread, randomly hand-sew 15 to 18 assorted-color seed beads on each tree. ▲

ABBREVIATIONS:	
ch(s)	chain(s)
Cl	cluster
dc	double crochet
sc	single crochet
Sh	shell
sl	slip
sp(s)	space(s)
st(s)	stitch(es)
tr	treble crochet
yo	yarn over

Craft Section...

Craft Christmas Fun...with Nutty Buddies

WHEN Renee Dent of Conrad, Montana took her unique Santas to the local Christmas bazaar, eager buyers snapped up every one. And that helped nurture a whole new holiday crop of the painted pals made from the same natural material—walnut shells!

Renee's quick and easy instructions for all four of her Christmasy characters follow. So get crackin'!

Materials Needed (for all ornaments):
Patterns on these two pages
Tracing paper
Pencil
No. 1 flat paintbrush
Tacky (white) glue
Satin spray finish
6-inch length of red pearl cotton for each ornament
English walnuts, carefully split in half (one-half needed for each ornament)
Plus see individual materials needed for each ornament.

Materials Needed (for Santa):
Acrylic paints—red, light pink, flesh, white and black
Shiny white dimensional fabric paint
2-inch x 2-1/2-inch piece of red felt
3/8-inch (9mm) white pom-pom
Iridescent glitter

Directions:
Referring to painting pattern, paint face and hat on walnut shell. Let dry, then spray with finish.

Apply tacky glue to hatband area and sprinkle with glitter. Use dimensional white paint to make Santa's mustache. Let dry several hours or overnight.

For hanger, fold 6-in. piece of pearl cotton in half and glue ends to top center back of walnut shell. For backing, glue back of shell to red felt. When dry, trim felt close to the edge of the shell.

Glue pom-pom to hat, referring to photo above for placement. Let dry.

Materials Needed (for elf):
Acrylic paints—green, red, light pink, flesh, white, brown and black
2-inch x 2-1/2-inch piece of red felt
6 inches of 1/8-inch-wide green satin ribbon
3/8-inch (9mm) red pom-pom

Directions:
Referring to painting pattern, paint face and hat on walnut shell. Let dry, then spray with finish.

Repeat Santa's directions for hanger and backing.

Tie a small bow with the green ribbon. Glue pom-pom to top of shell and bow under elf's chin, referring to photo above for placement. Let dry.

Materials Needed (for mouse angel):
Acrylic paints—gray, white and black
Felt—2-inch x 3-3/4-inch piece of gray and 1-1/2-inch square of pink
2-3/4 inches of white pearls-by-the-yard
6 inches of 1/8-inch-wide red satin ribbon

Directions:
Referring to painting pattern, paint walnut shell gray, then add face. Let dry, then spray with finish.

Repeat Santa's directions for hanger and backing, using gray felt piece for backing.

Trace outer ear and inner ear patterns onto tracing paper. Cut out two outer ears from gray felt and two inner ears from pink felt. Glue the pink felt pieces to the center of the gray felt pieces. Glue ears to the back of shell, checking photo for placement. Let dry.

For halo, make a circle with the string of pearls and glue closed to form the ha-lo. Let dry, then glue the halo to the mouse's head, tilting slightly as shown in photo above.

Tie a small bow with red ribbon. Glue bow under mouse's chin. Let dry.

Materials Needed (for Rudolph):
Acrylic paints—golden brown, white and black
2-inch x 2-1/2-inch pieces of both red and brown felt
3/8-inch (9mm) red pom-pom
6 inches of 1/8-inch-wide green satin ribbon
3/8-inch (9mm) jingle bell

Directions:
Referring to painting pattern, paint walnut shell golden brown, then add face. Let dry, then spray with finish.

Repeat Santa's directions for hanger and backing.

Trace antlers pattern onto tracing paper. Cut antlers from brown felt. Glue antlers to the back of the shell, referring to the photo for placement.

Glue red pom-pom onto face for nose.

Tie a small bow with the green ribbon. Glue bow, then bell to the top of Rudolph's head, referring to photo above for placement. Let dry. ▲

SANTA

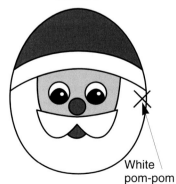

White pom-pom

Elegant But Easy, These Cherubs Trim the Tree

A FEW YARDS of yarn…a little lace …some scraps of cardboard…and hardly any time at all! There's not much more than that to adding these angels to your tree this Christmas.

Linda Whitener of Glen Allen, Missouri confides that you can craft an entire choir of the trims in minutes. "With a little supervision on the gluing part," she notes as well, "they're also a nifty project for little ones to do."

Materials Needed:

Small amount of white or off-white yarn (see note at end of article for using string instead)
Scraps of heavy cardboard
14 inches of 1-inch-wide white or off-white flat lace
2 inches of white pearls-by-the-yard
Scissors
Glue gun and glue sticks (use thick tacky glue if working with children)

Directions:

Cut a 6-in. x 2-in. piece of cardboard for wrapping the body and a 4-1/2-in. x 2-in. piece for wrapping the arms.

Cut eight pieces of yarn, each 10 in. long. Set aside.

BODY: Wrap the yarn 20 times lengthwise around the 6-in. piece of cardboard to form loops for the angel's body. Cut the yarn end so it is even with the edge of the cardboard.

Slip one piece of yarn between the cardboard and the loops at one end of the cardboard. Pull on both ends of the piece and tightly tie the piece into a knot. Repeat this step at the other end of the cardboard. Set aside.

ARMS: Wrap the yarn 15 times lengthwise around the 4-1/2-in. piece of cardboard to form loops for the angel's arms. Cut the yarn end so it is even with the edge of the cardboard. Tie a piece of yarn at each end of the cardboard as directed for the body.

Carefully slip the arm loops off of the 4-1/2-in. piece of cardboard. Tie a piece of yarn around the loops about 1/2 in. from the end to make a wrist. Tie another piece of yarn 1/2 in. from the other end of the loops. Cut these yarn ends to 1/2 in., then cut off the first knots you tied around each end of the arm loops.

ASSEMBLY: Carefully slip the body loops off of the 6-in. piece of cardboard. Tie a piece of yarn around the body 1 in. from the top knot of the loops, forming the neck. Trim yarn piece close to knot.

Slip the arm loops through the center of the body loops just below the neck. With arms pushed up to neck, tie a piece of yarn just below the arms to form the waist, about 1 in. to 1-1/4 in. below neck.

Cut the knot at the bottom of the body, cutting through the loops to form the angel's skirt.

Wings: Tie a bow in the 14-in. piece of lace and glue it centered onto the back just below the angel's neck.

Halo: Form a circle with the 2-in. length of pearls-by-the-yard and secure it with a bead of glue at the back of the angel's head.

Hanging loop: Pull the yarn piece tied at top of angel's head through the halo and tie a second knot 3 in. above her head. Cut yarn ends close to knot.

To use string: Follow the directions above, except wrap the string 60 times for the body and 45 times for the arms.

WALNUTTY ORNAMENTS PAINTING PATTERNS

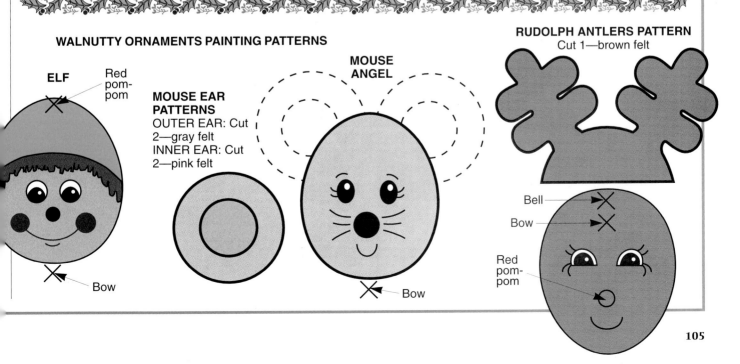

ELF
Red pom-pom
Bow

MOUSE EAR PATTERNS
OUTER EAR: Cut 2—gray felt
INNER EAR: Cut 2—pink felt

MOUSE ANGEL
Bow

RUDOLPH ANTLERS PATTERN
Cut 1—brown felt

Bell
Bow
Red pom-pom

Tiny Tomes Are Novel Way to Frame Favorite Family Photos

THESE crafty canvas book frames are sure to be best-sellers with your family—especially when you pop a precious picture inside!

Mary Cosgrove of Rockville, Connecticut shares her design for the simple plastic canvas project. It's one which results in frames that will speak volumes on your coffee table or fireplace mantel.

Materials Needed (for both frames):

Book frame charts on next page
Scraps or one 10-1/2-inch x 13-1/2-inch sheet of 7-count plastic canvas
Plastic canvas or worsted-weight yarn in colors listed on color key*
Two 12-inch lengths of Kreinik Heavy (#32) braid in Hi-Lustre Black or black worsted-weight yarn
Size 16 tapestry needle
Two 3-inch x 3-3/4-inch pieces of red solid fabric
Red thread and hand-sewing needle
Sharp craft scissors
Iron
Straight pins

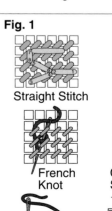

Invisible nylon thread (optional)
Two photos, each trimmed to 2-1/4 inches x 2-3/4 inches
*Mary used Needloft Plastic Canvas Yarn and Hi-Lustre Black Kreinik Heavy (#32) Braid.

Finished Size: Each frame is 2-3/4 inches wide x 3-1/2 inches tall.

Directions:

Making sure to count the bars and not the holes, cut three pieces of plastic canvas 18 bars wide x 23 bars high for each frame. For photo insert pieces, cut out center of one piece of plastic canvas for each frame, leaving four bars on all four sides as shown on chart on next page.

Cut 18-in. to 20-in. lengths of yarn. Follow charts and individual directions in next column to stitch each piece, referring to stitch illustrations in Fig. 1.

Do not knot yarn on back of work. Instead, leave a 1-in. tail on the back of the canvas and catch it in the first few stitches. To end this yarn and begin the next, run yarn ends under completed stitches on back of canvas, making sure to run under an area of matching color.

FRONTS: Work the front pieces of each frame in Continental stitch in colors indicated on charts, working details on each as directed below.

Santa: Add cross-stitches for his eyes with Black Kreinik Braid or black yarn and a French knot for his nose with red yarn.

Stocking: With yellow yarn, work cross-stitches for doll's braids, adding straight stitches for ends of braids. Work French knots for doll's eyes and nose with Black Kreinik Braid or black yarn.

PHOTO INSERTS/BACKS: Work photo insert and back pieces in slanted Gobelin stitches, using colors and direction indicated on charts. Overcast the inside edges of the photo insert pieces with white.

ASSEMBLY: Overcast and whipstitch all edges of each frame with red yarn as follows: Overcast right edge of photo insert pieces, left edge of back pieces and top, bottom and right edge of front pieces.

Holding wrong side of one photo insert to wrong side of one back piece, whipstitch the top and bottom edges, leaving an opening to insert a photo. Repeat for second frame.

Place the wrong side of the front piece on top of the appropriate photo insert/back unit and whipstitch the left edges together, working through all three layers.

Press under 1/4 in. on all edges of each red solid fabric piece. To cover the back of stitching, pin one piece to the wrong side of each trim front piece. Hand-stitch all edges of fabric piece to the wrong side of the front piece.

If desired, use nylon thread to make a loop for hanging, threading it through the top center of the frame (spine of the book) and knotting the ends together.

Slide a photo in between back and photo insert pieces on both frames. Since one side is left open, the photos can be changed from year to year. ▲

Fig. 1

Straight Stitch

Slanted Gobelin Stitch

French Knot

Continental Stitch

Cross-Stitch

Overcast and Whipstitch

STOCKING FRONT CHART
(Make 1—18 x 23 bars)

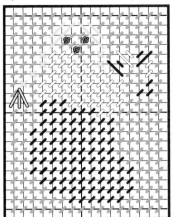

STOCKING BACK CHART
(Make 1—18 x 23 bars)

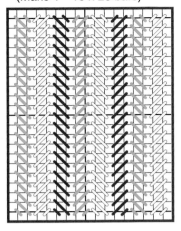

PHOTO INSERT CHART
(Make 2, 1 for each—18 x 23 bars)

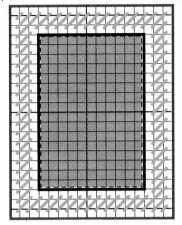

SANTA FRONT CHART
(Make 1—18 x 23 bars)

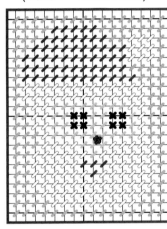

SANTA BACK CHART
(Make 1—18 x 23 bars)

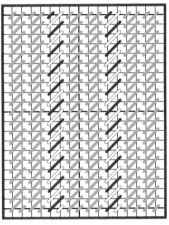

BOOK FRAMES

COLOR KEY	Needloft
✔ Christmas Red	02
✔ Pink	07
✔ Christmas Green	28
◯ White	41
✔ Yellow	57
✔ Black Kreinik Braid	005HL

FRENCH KNOTS

● Christmas Red	02
● Black Kreinik Braid	005HL

STRAIGHT STITCHES

⌏ Yellow	57

OVERCAST/WHIPSTITCH

— Christmas Red	02
— White	41

Cute Rudolph Brightens Up Yule Boughs

WITH this "endeering" ornament leading the way, children will see their way clear to a festive holiday. Designer Rosalie Sheptick of Hayward, Wisconsin devised the quick and easy craft that turns a burned-out bulb into a beaming bit of cheer.

With Rosalie's illuminating instructions, Brownie or Cub Scout troops and 4-H groups can round up a herd of these terrific tree trimmers in no time!

Materials Needed:
Used red Christmas tree light bulb
Two 1/4-inch (6mm) movable eyes
8-inch piece of brown pipe cleaner or chenille stem for antlers
3/4-inch red pom-pom for nose
Sequins in holly shape for decorations on antlers
Tacky (white) glue
6-inch length of 1/4-inch red satin ribbon for hanger

Directions:
Wind the pipe cleaner around the top of the Christmas bulb, twisting it in the front to secure. Referring to the photo at right, bend the two ends of the pipe cleaner to make the antlers.

Referring to photo, glue movable eyes, then pom-pom nose onto bulb. Let dry.

Glue the holly sequins onto the twist-ed center of the antlers. Let dry.

For hanger, fold ribbon in half and overhand-knot ends together. Glue center of ribbon to top of bulb, holding in place until glue sets. ▲

Quilts Hung on Tree Are Eye-Catching Ornaments

"COLORFULLY COUNTRY" will certainly describe your family's Christmas tree when you add these cross-stitched quilt block ornaments to your store of holiday decor! The homespun threesome works well as package toppers, too, assures designer Michele Crawford of Spokane, Washington.

Materials Needed (for all three ornaments):

Charts on next page
Three 4-1/4-inch squares of Zweigart 14-count Hearthstone Aida cloth (No. 053 Parchment)
Three 4-1/4-inch squares of red Christmas print fabric
J&P Coats or Anchor six-strand embroidery floss in colors listed on color key
Coats Dual Duty Plus Thread—one spool each of 128A Atom Red, 177 Kerry Green and 256 Natural
Coats Bias Corded Piping—one package each of 128A Atom Red and 177 Kerry Green
Anchor Marlitt—one skein each of

No. 843 (Red), No. 1037 (Beige) and No. 812 (Green)
Three 1-1/4-inch-tall novelty or ceramic buttons of your choice*
Small amount of raffia
Polyester stuffing
Water-soluble fabric marker
Ruler
Standard sewing supplies

*Michele used ceramic buttons—a snowman, candy cane and gingerbread man—for her ornaments.

Finished Size: Each ornament measures about 3-3/4 inches square. Design area of each ornament is 42 stitches wide x 42 stitches high.

Directions:

CROSS-STITCHING: Zigzag or overcast edges of Aida cloth to prevent fraying. Fold each piece in half lengthwise, then fold in half crosswise to determine center and mark this point with water-soluble marker. To find center of chart, draw lines across chart connecting arrows. Begin stitching at this point so design will be centered.

Separate the floss and use two strands for cross-stitching and for back-stitching hearts. Use one strand for backstitching quilting lines on Designs 2 and 3. (See Fig. 1 on next page.)

Each symbol on chart equals one stitch over a set of fabric threads with different symbols representing different colors or stitches. Make stitches in the colors shown on the chart or in colors of your choice, first completing all cross-stitching, then backstitching.

Do not knot floss on back of work. Instead, leave a short tail on back of work and hold in place. Weave tails and ends through several stitches as stitching progresses.

Hand-sew a novelty or ceramic button in the center of each stitched quilt block.

ASSEMBLY: After stitching is completed, cut trim edges from each stitched design, leaving nine sets of threads beyond the outside of each design. Round corners slightly.

With right sides together and raw edges matching, use Kerry Green thread, a zipper foot and a 1/4-in. seam allowance to baste the green corded piping around the edges of Design 1 as follows: Begin by angling the piping from the edge of the fabric over to the seamline as in Fig. 2 on next page, stitching on top of the baste-stitching of the piping. Before sewing around each corner, clip the seam allowance of the piping, then ease in extra on each corner. Angle piping off at the end.

Repeat this step on Designs 2 and 3, using Atom Red thread and red corded piping.

Center a stitched square on a fabric square, right sides together. Trim edges and corners of fabric squares to match stitched squares.

Use matching thread to stitch each ornament together on all sides, leaving a 2-in. opening on one side of each. Trim corners. Turn right side out. Lightly stuff. Fold in opening edges and hand-stitch openings closed.

Tie three 1-1/2-in. raffia bows and sew one to the top center of each stuffed ornament using Natural thread.

Hanging Loop: Cut three 14-in. lengths of each color of Marlitt. Bring one length of each color together to make three sets. Tie an overhand knot at the end of each set of lengths. Braid each set of Marlitt.

Fold one braided length in half. Sew folded center of the Marlitt to top center back of one ornament. Tie ends together in an overhand knot for a 4-in.-long hanging loop. Repeat this step to complete the other two ornaments. ▲

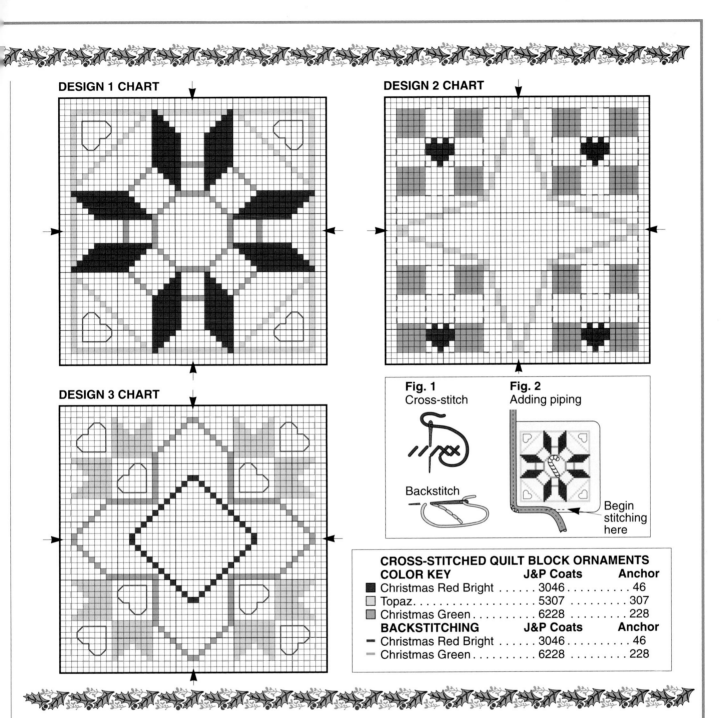

DESIGN 1 CHART

DESIGN 2 CHART

DESIGN 3 CHART

Fig. 1
Cross-stitch

Backstitch

Fig. 2
Adding piping

Begin
stitching
here

CROSS-STITCHED QUILT BLOCK ORNAMENTS

COLOR KEY	J&P Coats	Anchor
Christmas Red Bright	3046	46
Topaz	5307	307
Christmas Green	6228	228
BACKSTITCHING	**J&P Coats**	**Anchor**
Christmas Red Bright	3046	46
Christmas Green	6228	228

Holiday Tip...
Christmas Cards Are a Snap to Her

I'VE FOUND a fast and easy way to use my hobby, photography, to make the holidays merrier for family and friends ...with *personalized* Christmas cards I put together.

When I take a snapshot I especially like, I get several extra copies printed. I also keep a selection of fold-over linen-finish notecards in a variety of colors on hand.

Then, when the holidays come along, I choose an appropriate picture and make my own customized greeting card—one as pretty as any you'd find in a stationery store!

Using spray mount adhesive, I glue the photo onto the front of the notecard. Since the inside of the card is blank, I compose my own message. Sometimes, I include a poem as part of my greeting.

Both the notecards (with matching envelopes) and adhesive can be purchased at craft and art supply stores.

And, now that I have a large range of subjects, I've discovered another way to share my "line" of cards—making up blank sets to give as gifts!

—*Janet Rose Lehmberg*
Monsey, New York

Editor's Note: *Country Woman readers got a peek through Janet's lens in the Cooks' Outlooks feature in the May/June 1990 issue. Since then, her work has been published in her local newspaper and featured on a calendar. She's also won an award in a contest sponsored by the U.S. Department of Agriculture.*

Potter's Creations Make Merry Little Christmas

GOOD THINGS come in small packages with Lynne Gilbert. This time of year, the Pennsylvania potter has her hands full…crafting over 500 mini ornaments to brighten holiday boughs!

"When I started making my redware back in '85, my aim was to make something that children could afford to give as Christmas gifts," she recalls from her rural Bechtelsville home in the heart of Pennsylvania Dutch Country.

Although Lynne also creates a variety of larger tree trimmers (several hundred a year!) and decorative plates with historically accurate designs, the delicate quarter-sized ornaments still make up the bulk of her output.

"A mini feather tree is the right place for my small ornaments," she notes. "They're snapped up by people who want a traditional Pennsylvania German Christmas look."

The first step for Lynne in fashioning her "cookie cutter" ornaments or plates is rolling out the clay with a rolling pin and forming the shape. From there, she chooses the decorating technique best suited to the piece.

Some of Lynne's mini redware ornaments are made by a process called slip trailing, where the design is drawn on with white or colored "slip", a paint-like substance, trailed from a fine-tipped container.

But most of the ornaments and plates are decorated by "sgraffito". "White slip is applied to leather-hard clay and a design is drawn on with pencil," she explains. "The pencil lines are scratched over with a tool that removes the white layer to reveal the red clay under it."

Once the design is finished, Lynne fires the pieces, then applies color and glaze—a step that sometimes attracts aid from Lynne's feline "assistants".

"My mom's cat has been 'helping' since he was a kitten," she laughs. "And, while I don't work on pottery at my home much, my cat, 'Lucky', is also a 'potter cat'. He loves to watch me work…and steal my brushes."

With Christmas on the way and trees awaiting their tiny trims, here's hoping she keeps some extras close at hand!

Editor's Note: *For information on custom orders, contact Lynne at Redware Whimsey, 2138 Old Rt. 100, Bechtelsville PA 19505; 1-610/845-7410.* ▲

MERRY MINIATURES (above and left) make historic holiday looks for collectors, thanks to steady hand of potter Lynne Gilbert (inset left). Details delight on Christmas-themed plates.

Wreaths Ring in Happy Holidays!

Christmas comes full circle for country crafters from coast to coast. The proof's in all these well-rounded handmades that merrily deck halls, doors and walls.

COWBOY CHRISTMAS. Betty Blagg, Waterford, California, lassos holiday cheer with rope wreath that's home on range—paper twist bow, bandanna, calf bell round out look.

HOLIDAY'S BEARY MERRY for Sidney Gosnell. Festive teddies greet guests from front door of longtime bear collector's home in Enid, Oklahoma. She even decks out a special tree indoors with lights in shape of her favorite furry friends!

MITTEN MOTIF. Ellen Fjermedal has season well in hand with rosemaling ornaments she painted on handmade grapevine wreath at Brooklyn, New York home. Her husband cuts out seasonal shapes and she adds festive finishing touches.

YARNING for the holidays, Gloria Beane, Bingham, Maine, turns pom-poms and hanger into fluffy festive finery. Santa is the center of attention in her Christmasy crafting creations.

NUTS for Christmas? Take a tip from Regina Herring and get crackin'! Natural wreath of pinecones, nuts and berries tastefully decorates her Fairfax, Virginia home for holidays.

The Country Christmas That Took Us for a Ride

By D. Bauer of Lucinda, Pennsylvania

rowing up on our family farm half a century ago, I enjoyed many merry Christmases. Of them, none was more memorable than one that truly "transported" me, my brothers and my sisters.

It began in the usual way. The day before, my older brothers cut a tree from the hillside below the barn. Its destination was our all-purpose gathering room, the only room besides the kitchen in our farmhouse kept heated in winter.

That night, we all piled into the 1930 Chevy. Like most cars of its vintage, of course, it had no heater, so we shivered as we putt-putted up the road to attend midnight Mass.

Christmas morning, the festive focus turned to food—and not just ours! Mum made towers of buckwheat cakes, loaded two frying pans with sausage patties and fried dozens of eggs. In addition, all the animals enjoyed a treat. We served up extra corn for the cows, oats for the horses, milk for the barn cats and bacon rind or sausage for the dogs.

(This prompted one of Mum's favorite sayings. If there happened to be extra table scraps anytime during the year, she always remarked, "The cats will think it's Christmas!")

Like many families of the time, ours never had much money. We children didn't dare dream about expensive toys, bicycles, radios or watches. The presents we received were usually practical ones—school clothes, warm hats and gloves—plus a single small toy or game for each of us. All the same, we considered ourselves fortunate. When you don't have much to begin with, *anything* new is special.

This particular year, however, we got a big surprise that would be the highlight of our holiday celebrations for Christmases to come—a brand-new sled Dad built just for us!

The sled had hand-carved wooden runners that curved up in the back and a bar in front for steering with a rope. Best of all, it came with two thick interchangeable oak planks—one 5 feet long and one 12 feet long. With the latter, we could make room for whoever wanted to come along for the ride!

We couldn't wait to try out our present. First, though, we needed to "fuel up".

As she did each year once we were through opening gifts, Mum brought out her silver-covered chocolate drops and ribbon candy. She warned us not to eat too much or we'd spoil our dinner—as if *anything* could spoil the feast she worked so hard to prepare for us.

For our big meal, Mum served chicken, mashed potatoes and cream gravy, turnips, coleslaw, home-canned carrots plus pickles and beets. Her golden-brown spicy-flavored pumpkin pie made the perfect dessert.

That afternoon, nearly numb from all we'd eaten, we bundled up and waddled outside to take our sled on its maiden voyage.

Up across the railroad tracks we stomped, pulling the sled behind. Our gum boots made ridged tracks in the fresh snow, and our breath formed icy droplets on the scarves we knotted tight across our frozen noses. It was a long cold time until we reached the top of the hill.

As soon as we scaled the height, though, we scrambled aboard—every one of us at once. The person in back clung to the one in front and tucked his or her feet in the lap ahead. Then…*whoosh*—the breathtaking descent began!

Swooping down the icy hill along with the rest of us, our hearts and stomachs seemed to drop to our frozen toes before rising into our throats. We looked for all the world like one long wool-coated snow-covered caterpillar.

With the wooden plank creaking and the runners squeaking, we picked up speed. Snow flew all around us, turning our clothes white, a sharp contrast to our chilly red faces.

The twin bump-bump as we zoomed across the railroad tracks bounced off half the load. Lightened, the sled coasted even faster to the bottom of the hill. Finally, it came to a stop near the Hoovers' mailbox.

Everyone rolled off, laughing and sputtering as we dug ice out of our boots and sleeves.

Difficult as it would have been to believe just a short time before, the long sled ride had burned off Mum's delicious feast…and we were actually hungry again. Knowing we'd have plenty of time for more white-knuckle trips down the hill, we trooped back home to snatch cold chicken off the platter in the pantry and cut slabs of pie from the tins near the window.

(Mum never had to cook an evening meal on Christmas Day—everyone just ate up the leftovers and filled in the hollows with bread!)

In the years to come, there would be more fondly remembered Christmases in my life. But a *better* one? Not yet! ▲

May the beauty of the season remain with you and yours the whole year through.

INDEX

Share Your Country Christmas with Us!

WE WOULD love to hear how you make Christmastime shine for your family and friends. We may even be able to feature you in a future *Country Woman Christmas*!

Do you have an interesting assortment of Christmas collectibles? Or do you decorate for the holidays in a festive way?

Perhaps you have an outstanding *original* recipe or craft you'd like to share. (We would need to see a good-quality photo of the craft project.)

Maybe you own a Christmas-related country business...or know of a Christmas-loving country woman other folks might like to meet. If so, please let us know.

Don't forget to include the holiday family pictures and nostalgic stories that make your memories merry.

Please send your ideas to "CW Christmas Book", 5925 Country Lane, Greendale WI 53129. (Enclose a self-addressed stamped envelope if you would like your materials to be returned.)